LEND TO LIVE

LEND
to
Live

Earn Hassle-Free Passive Income
in Real Estate
with Private Money Lending

BY ALEXANDRIA BRESHEARS
AND BETH PINKLEY JOHNSON

BiggerPockets®
PUBLISHING
Denver, Colorado

Praise for
LEND TO LIVE

"As the oldest and largest national association for the profession of private lending, we receive frequent requests from individuals about where and how to start. We are ecstatic that we can now offer a simple direction: Start your private lending journey with *Lend to Live* in hand.

Authors Alex and Beth approach this nuanced vocation with practical, clear, and complete guidance that seeks neither to overcomplicate nor oversimplify the variables involved."

—The American Association of Private Lenders

"If *Lend To Live* was published before I started lending money ten years ago, I would have saved over $50,000 in problematic loan costs… I'm shocked at how simple Alex and Beth made the lending process while still keeping all the important nuances needed to be successful in this business. If you are currently lending money, considering lending money, or even raising capital for your own real estate deals from private lenders, this is a MUST-READ!"

—Bill Allen, Owner/CEO, 7 Figure Flipping

"Alex and Beth have put together a helpful guide on private lending that takes a truly unique approach to the subject. Their thoughtfulness and personal experiences shine light on what can at times be an overwhelming process so even a brand new lender can follow along."

—Melissa Martorella, Partner, Geraci LLP

Lend to Live: Earn Hassle-Free Passive Income in Real Estate with Private Money Lending
Alexandria Breshears and Beth Pinkley Johnson

Published by BiggerPockets Publishing LLC, Denver, CO
Copyright © 2022 by Alexandria Breshears and Beth Pinkley Johnson
All rights reserved.

Publisher's Cataloging-in-Publication Data
Names: Breshears, Alexandria Imogen, 1980- author. | Johnson, Bethany Pinkley, 1975- author.
Title: Lend to live : earn hassle-free passive income in real estate with private money lending / Alexandria Breshears and Beth Johnson.
Description: Denver, CO: BiggerPockets Publishing, LLC, 2022.
Identifiers: LCCN: 2022932992 | ISBN: 9781947200708 (paperback) | 9781947200715 (ebook)
Subjects: LCSH Real estate investment--Finance. | Women in real estate. | BISAC BUSINESS & ECONOMICS / Real Estate / Mortgages | BUSINESS & ECONOMICS / Investments & Securities / Real Estate | BUSINESS & ECONOMICS / Real Estate / General | BUSINESS & ECONOMICS / Women in Business
Classification: LCC HD1382.5 .B74 2022 | DDC 332.63/24--dc23

Published in the United States of America
10 9 8 7 6 5 4 3 2 — 1

DEDICATION

Alex

This book is dedicated to my chosen family, who continue to be my inspiration and motivation in everything I do. I also dedicate this to all those who have walked the path before me, and to those who will follow after. Never forget we can accomplish more together than we ever could individually.

Beth

This book could not have happened without my husband, Matt. Without you, none of this would matter. I also dedicate this book to my parents, who taught me just about everything I know in real estate; you didn't just invest in real estate, you invested in your family's future. Finally, for my children—both by birth and by choice. Caleb, Rachel, and Mia, you give me purpose. There is absolutely nothing I wouldn't do for my family.

TABLE OF CONTENTS

AUTHORS' PREFACE

BETH

Though my journey to become a private lender was an accidental one, my childhood was rich with peripheral experiences in real estate investing. My father was a woodshop teacher in middle school, and my mother stayed at home to raise five kids. Realizing my father was not going to get wealthy as a teacher, my parents delved into real estate as a young couple, buying, rehabbing, and renting or selling well before "flipping" was even a term.

They never disclosed their capital sources or project financials, but my sister and I would tag along on weekends and after school to watch my dad do much of the work himself along with my brothers' help. We'd listen to our Walkmans and pick up shingles and nails in the yard or sweep freshly demoed bedrooms—whatever my dad thought would keep us out of trouble. I loathed those weekends, because I was unable to do as I wished and had to spend most of my nonschool hours in what I thought was a complete waste of my playtime.

While I had zero appreciation for those experiences back then—and I truly mean zero—I now understand the types of skills, the purposefulness, and the education my parents were trying to instill in us while creating generational wealth for our entire family. Today, three out of five of my siblings own real estate–related businesses. I knew, just like my dad, I would have some sort of real estate side hustle while climbing the corporate-America ladder after college. In my mid-20s, I started with my first live-in flip and cashed in on my small improvements (and some healthy appreciation) after two years and one week—with no capital gains! It was the biggest check I'd ever seen, and I was ready to do it again!

Then life happened. I got married, worked a full-time job with increasing roles and responsibilities, and started planning for a family. Flipping on the side became more difficult as my energy and spare time whittled down to almost nothing. My priorities shifted overnight when I suddenly lost my mother just weeks after telling her of my first pregnancy. She was so excited that her baby (I am the youngest of five children) was finally having a baby. Family was everything to her. Shortly after, with a live-in flip and another flip project in progress, I found myself—pregnant, tired, and in mourning—on all fours painting trim boards and wondering what really mattered most to me. My mother had told me so often over the decades to work hard and play later, which was a piece of advice she was never able to see through. She was a young 62 years old when she passed away suddenly.

Nine months later in January 2008, after my son Caleb was born, I found I lacked the drive to continue working an 8-to-5 job. I was also holding a couple of real estate projects that brought me little joy, especially as the market started to show signs of weakness. I found I needed my mom's sage advice more than ever. It was at this point in my life when I decided my career aspirations, purely egocentric ambitions at best, were no longer important. I wanted to stay at home with my son as long as I could, because it was time I would never get back.

You might think this is the point in my story where I tell you I began my adventure into private lending as a means of creating passive income sources so I could stay home. It certainly seems like the perfect timing in my story to do so. But it wasn't. Because life throws us curveballs. We find ourselves in situations, with people, in places, we never thought we'd be, thinking to ourselves, *How the hell did I get here?* At least, I did. Maybe you were lucky enough to escape the pain of a troubled relationship to teach you a few life lessons. Not me.

After ten years and two babies, I became a single mom and worked part-time as a consultant for a large technology company in Redmond, Washington. I wasn't focused on the future. I was squarely in the present, just living day-to-day and being there for my kids. This was my time to simply enjoy life in peace, seeing as I couldn't for so long before then. I was determined to make a life for myself and my kids.

However, it was on one of my first dates postdivorce that I met my future husband, Matt Flynn. After a few dates, he casually mentioned wanting to get into private lending again. We discussed real estate a lot when we were together, so not wanting to come across as obtuse, I played along like I understood what he was talking about. I went home later one night and googled the term since I'd never even heard it before. I'd be lying if I said I was intrigued by it. Truthfully, I wasn't in the headspace to think about real estate hustles again.

A few months later when the opportunity arose to help Matt find private lending opportunities, I immediately said yes. Why not earn a few extra bucks helping him while we enjoyed each other's company? It also appealed to me because I could assist him from home, on my own schedule, around my children's needs.

So why do I feel compelled to tell you my life story? Because most of us can relate to finding ourselves in life situations we never expected—both good and bad. These moments prompt us to start thinking differently about how we want to live our lives. Perhaps you experienced a social outing where your friend told you about his private lending and how he's making money passively for his family's future. Or maybe you have a colleague you used to work with who left her corporate day job to start a career in real estate investing. Working mothers like me, especially single moms, probably understand the dire need I had to break free of my day job and create more freedom for myself and my kids. But how?

For me, those pivotal moments were losing my mother in my early 30s and realizing my career would never define me again, and a clandestine conversation over copious amounts of wine about the income potential associated with the world of private lending. I imagine you picked up this book because you also had some sort of realization that private lending might be able to provide you with personal and financial independence without the hassle of being a landlord or flipper.

In this book, my business partner, Alex, and I want to speak directly to those of you seeking more personal flexibility. More financial independence. An ability to do whatever and go wherever your mind (and body) takes you in the moment. As working women who have struggled with our identities outside our professional images and sought more balance to our chaotic personal lives, we want to share our stories and the journeys we took to become private lenders. For both of us, private lending became our much-needed lifelines to personal freedom.

Consider this book a "business in a backpack" that you can take wherever you go. Need to review a loan opportunity from a prospective borrower? You can do it from your phone at soccer practice. Want to make passive income while you spend a month traveling across Europe? You can do that too. Perhaps you want to generate an income replacement to help you achieve your goals of retiring early from your soul-sucking day job. Private lending will not only allow you this latitude, but it can also financially facilitate it as well. All you need is the desire to create change for yourself and your family, a computer with internet access, email, and a cell phone. Other than that, you need very little in that backpack of yours besides perhaps sunscreen and any other personal provisions you may prefer.

As you read through this book, please consider a few things that brought my business partner and I to where we are today. First, why do you want to enter private lending and what outcomes are you seeking? Most the of time it isn't strictly about money but about the lifestyle you desire. Understanding your own motivations will help you choose what your private lending adventure will look like. Maybe it's a few loans a year so you travel more or contribute passively to your family's income. Maybe it's eventually starting a full-blown private lending practice, like I suddenly found myself doing, so you can quit your day job. Or maybe you just want to utilize private lending as a diversification strategy in your investments. Whatever the "why" may be, make sure you know what that is and keep it top of mind as you read this book and embark on your journey into private lending. If not, you could find yourself overwhelmed from actively managing your investments rather than enjoying the passive source of income that drew you to private lending in the first place.

Second, make sure you truly understand what your approach is to investments of all shapes and sizes. What is your risk tolerance, what keeps you up at night, and what goals are you seeking from private lending as an income source? As a person who leans toward high anxiety levels, I prefer lower-risk deals and will lower my interest rates accordingly for those no-brainer types of loan opportunities. But I have met people who say they don't get out of bed for anything less than 13 percent annualized returns and will assume higher risk for those deals. Figure out where you fall on the spectrum of risk versus reward and keep that as a beacon for your decisions.

Whatever the case may be for you, the introspective aspect to private lending is something we cannot dictate for you. We can share with you the key steps to funding a loan in a safe and secure way, but we cannot help you decide the appropriate risks for you to take and what your personal decision-making should look like. To aid your self-discovery, we have a tool kit on our website (www.biggerpockets.com/lendingbonus) that will help you better understand your personal journey to private lending. Throughout the book, we'll reference tools and resources available to help you personalize your key learnings.

As you delve into the world of private lending, we'd love to hear about your progress along the way. Much like new moms who lack perspective on how to handle a baby who won't sleep through the night, new lenders need a support system to help them work through tough situations, explore the *what-ifs*, and celebrate little successes. My more experienced mom friends were my lifeline, especially since my mom was not around to help guide me through motherhood gracefully. It truly takes a village, and each and every story you share helps others gain perspective that they otherwise would not have available to them.

On that note, we've woven personal stories from our network throughout this book to provide additional points of view that can help shape your own private lending storyline. Hopefully, these stories—the good, the bad, and the ugly—will help give you the confidence you need to get started in building passive income through private lending, and serve as cautionary tales of what not to do along the way.

Though you may be reading (or listening) to this book while your child takes a nap or in the evening after a hard day's work, our hope is you will soon be able to create a future lifestyle you desire. Eventually you can read more books and fund more loans from any seat you want, whether it's a beach chair or the driver's seat of a car while sitting in the rain waiting for your kids to get out of school, like I am doing right now. While the latter may not be super sexy, it's a luxury of choice many do not receive and are not able to give themselves. Private lending has afforded me this privilege and, in time, will for you as well. Cheers to what's to come!

ALEX

Like many people, my journey to private lending was not a linear progression of a calculated plan or steps. Sometimes I wish there was a plan or a step, or even a manual, but that would take a bit of the adventure out of it. My accidental introduction to private lending started at a real estate investment association (REIA) meeting almost twenty years ago. Being the outgoing, never-met-a-stranger-type of person I am, I struck up a conversation with someone standing next to me at the event. It turns out he ran what he termed a "hard-money loan business," and he was looking for help! I had no idea what I was getting into. All I knew was that he said the magic words every college student wants to hear: "You can work your own hours." I was sold!

I worked in the office processing checks, going out into the city collecting applications, and walking through subject properties. Remember, this was back before phones were smart, and the easiest way to get written information to someone was to fax it. Lending looks much different now! Since this was a small operation, I was also the person collecting those wonderful interest-only payments every month and hand delivering them to the bank at the end of each workday. After a few months, I started noticing a trend. Borrowers would come in, often stressed, lamenting some problem at the property related to bad tenants or contractors (or both!), but they still showed up at the office to pay their mortgage. Meanwhile, the owner of the lending business was often out on the golf course or at lunch with a friend or colleague. I saw the contrast between the active investors coming in—stressed from managing a rehab or fresh off an encounter with an unpleasant tenant—and the lender I worked for. While the investors stressed, week after week I was depositing checks between $700 and $2,700 in the lender's business bank account.

I also frequently attended local landlord meetups during this time. I am someone who has a passion for learning, so if you invite me to learn something new, I'll likely take you up on it. Again, a trend emerged when I was talking to landlords. The market I was in at the time was not a cash flowing market, but more of an appreciation market. Landlords appeared to cross their fingers that the tenants paid, then spent the rest of the 29 days of the month hoping nothing broke, all to claim their $100 to $200 a month "profit" from the property. I saw them rationalize this away with their mumblings about "depreciation" on their taxes and their building equity in the property. A saying that is famous in real estate and something the lender I worked for said often was "You can't eat equity." This rang through my head whenever I heard landlords mention their equity gains from appreciation and capital paydown. Granted, this was the early 2000s, and as many saw in 2008—especially in Florida, where these conversations took place—their equity vanished quickly and in some cases put them underwater on their investments. Life isn't about telling people what you know; it is about listening to what others think they know and applying that to your own life or belief system. These early conversations and observations shaped my view of investing in real estate for years to come.

Like Beth, I had plans, but it's called "life" and not "dress rehearsal" for a reason. I was in college as a chemistry major, hell-bent on going to vet school to become an equine vet. My happy place was a barn. Again, listening to the people around me taught me more than I ever learned in a classroom. I worked evenings and weekends at a very high-end barn. These horses were bought and sold for more than the home I lived in at the time. I was "the help" and often not referred to by name. I was simply asked when or if I was going to do something for their horse. One owner befriended me, as her horse required special medical care and daily treatments in the evening. One afternoon, as I was pulling up to get my day started, she asked if I would run to get her some cold drinks. She tossed the keys to her luxury SUV at me, handed me a $100 bill, and told me to keep the change. Fortunately, I'm somewhat tall for a woman or else my jaw would have hit the floor. About thirty minutes later I came back with drinks, her change, and her car in one piece. I attempted to hand her the change, feeling guilty for keeping $75 to run to the corner store and back. She waved if off and told me to keep it, she didn't need it. This owner was at the barn every day, frequently in the middle of the day, no less. That afternoon I got the courage to ask her what she did for a living that allowed her to be at the barn in the middle of the day. She told me she owned real estate and owned notes on homes. I didn't know what that latter part meant, but I was going to find out!

About a year after this I married an active-duty service member and life got crazy with moves across the country, sometimes with only two weeks' notice! We ended up accidental landlords twice, sold one of the homes as a fix-and-flip, and kept the second, hoping to move back into it "someday." We were not prepared to be landlords from 3,000 miles away, despite hiring a property management company. Toward the end of the twelve-month lease, I dreaded picking up my cell phone because it would undoubtedly be a call from the tenants telling me there was yet another problem with the house (mostly tenant caused) or that they wanted their rent to be lowered or paid late without penalty (again). For years we moved from state to state, time zone to time zone. We never bought another home and refused to have long-term rentals again. We were burned. If that was what real estate investing meant, both my husband and I were not going to be real estate investors. That was a miserable life for us!

Fast-forward about fifteen years, and again the idea of investing popped up. Technology and access to information had greatly improved, so remote investing was more common. Through all our travels, we made friends with other military members who were also interested in real estate. We had been stationed in a lot of the same markets and knew many of the same people and limitations that military life puts on people. I came across someone who needed capital to finish renovations on an investment property to get it ready to sell. Within a month we were lenders on that investment, collecting small interest-only checks as we took a second lien out on that home. It was thrilling to get that first interest-only check from the borrower! It made me remember my first job in real estate working with the lender so many years ago. This got my mind racing: *This may be a way for me to build a business for myself as a military spouse, one that could travel with me wherever we go!* I just had to pick a market I knew well, and had connections in, then learn about that market and lending laws. It was easy. Or so I thought.

It turns out there wasn't much demand on YouTube back then to explain how to do a private loan.

This information deficit was something I faced time and again when it came to private lending. It was almost the voodoo of real estate: Everyone knew it existed and could put a name to it, but only a select few knew how to do it, and no one ever talked about it. Short of hiring an attorney who you thought knew about lending in real estate, you had no real way to learn more about what was possible, commonplace, or truly legal. Little by little, the pieces of the puzzle fell into place. We continued to do these one-off loans every so often but never considered it a way to make a full-time living. We didn't know what we didn't know, so throwing ourselves into that abyss didn't seem the most prudent path of progression.

Then the global pandemic hit in 2020. The world literally shut down. Neighbors waved at one another from a distance, talking was done via video calls, and family members visited one another through glass. As a military family, we were used to being disconnected geographically from family, but now we weren't even allowed to travel to see them. We were hesitant to visit with our friends in our local area, even if everyone sat outside, 6 feet apart. It forced this extrovert inside. When that happened, I looked for people, for community. Of course, still interested in investing, I went looking for the lending community. By now, I thought, technology had to have evolved to create more open and honest conversations about lending. I was wrong. Every social media group I joined that had "private lending" or "lending" in the title turned out to be a place for scams and spam. There wasn't any networking or education-based conversation taking place. Where were my people?

At the same time, the global pandemic had another side effect that created the perfect storm for my jump into "full-time" private lending. Many hard-money lenders totally shut their doors, their funding drying up as the cases of the virus climbed. This left investors with little recourse but to find another source of capital or miss out on a deal. The military community being as close-knit as we are, a service member connected with me in one of those "Zoom breakout rooms" that now seem like a daily occurrence. The universe put the person, environment, and opportunity together for me to fund this loan. We were off to the races as "real" private lenders, business LLC and all. I felt like I knew what I was doing, but I had only just hit the tip of the iceberg. Diving in and making private lending my one thing has taught me that the education never stops. No matter your experience, you can always learn a new tidbit to help your business—something you never thought of before or even knew existed.

While finally ready to take this challenge on full-time, I lamented not having a community or a mentor to talk to or ask questions. I bought nearly every book out there on private lending, but they varied from commercial to encyclopedic in terms of reading quality. It wasn't until I started connecting with other private lenders that the real learning began.

The more investors and lenders I spoke with, the more the same recurring themes kept coming up. No one knew where to start, how to structure things, what to look out for, or even how to meet one another. Active investors wanted rates and terms from private individuals like they were a bank, and individuals were asking for every piece of documentation from borrowers without any clue how to read them. Or worse, lenders asked for no paperwork for due diligence and only found out about serious problems or outright fraud after the money left their accounts. It was one thing to learn to make myself and my family more prosperous, but quite another to stand on the sidelines and watch others lose out. An offhanded remark by a friend telling me to start a group if I couldn't find one turned out to be the single greatest piece of advice I could have received. I started the group not knowing a thing about marketing, graphic design, social media algorithms, or even the basics of branding. I found some photos I liked, came up with a catchy name, and ten minutes later there was a group. I didn't think much of it until there were one hundred people in the group only one week later! *Uh oh... Now what am I going to do?!*

So I found a speaker for the group to present on a topic I myself was wanting to learn more about anyway. We had eight attendees at that first presentation, including myself and the speaker. Six people showed up to hear what he had to say. Step by step, little by little, the group grew, as did the connections being made, the knowledge being shared, and the respect for private lending itself. A little more than a year later, the group had grown to 6,000 participants without any advertising or marketing.

Like I said in the beginning: I wish there was a plan that laid out all of these things, but that just isn't the case. One step leads to another, which leads you to a third. You just keep going. The journey you are about to embark on is a product of that random choice on that one day and the thousands of decisions that played out after it. If you ask me, there wasn't a single extraordinary thing I did other than listen and have a heart with a desire to help. I truly believe that if I can do it, anyone can do it. It didn't take hours of time to execute, I had professionals helping along the way, and while there was a learning curve, it did level out and become a lot more fun by the end. What you are holding in your hand is the journey in condensed form. Let this be a framework, a guiding light, and an opportunity to widen your horizons on investing in real estate. It isn't all just farmhouse sinks in ugly houses or dealing with tenants, toilets, and trashed units. Private lending fit my lifestyle, my personality, and my skill set. Most importantly, it provided passive income I wanted. These pages are not only an introduction on how to do private lending more safely but also a chance to consider your goals, your why, and what you genuinely enjoy doing. The journey will be infinitely longer than the destination, so why not enjoy the ride?

DISCLAIMER:

We want to be very up front about a few things about this book. First, neither of us are financial advisors, tax professionals, or lawyers. The information we are sharing in this book represents a culmination of our personal experiences in the lending space, and the most current process and our interpretations of the laws as they are at the time of publication. Use this information for educational purposes and consult the appropriate professional with any questions about your specific financial or legal concerns.

Chapter 1
THE WHO AND THE HOW

The goal of this book is to reveal to you the wealth-building power of private lending. The realm of borrowing and repaying doesn't have to exist solely in the hallowed halls of Wall Street investment funds or the local conglomerate bank. In fact, private lending is frequently done by individuals just like you. With the knowledge in this book, you can accomplish this style of investing more safely and with enough dedication to generate a dependable stream of income for yourself and your family.

WHO SHOULD READ THIS BOOK

Most people assume you only need to learn about private lending if you are actively going into this type of investment as an individual lender. However, there are many advantages to becoming more familiar with private lending concepts and best practices. Whether you are an active real estate investor, a passive investor such as a landlord, or a limited partner in a private debt fund, understanding the basics and learning how to navigate the private lending process will help all parties involved in ensuring a smooth real estate investment transaction.

The Active Investor

Flippers, developers, and other active real estate investors are continuously on the hunt for the next deal and know that searching for the capital to fund those deals is a constant activity. Being able to find and court high-net-worth individuals to fund future projects is critical to maintaining consistent deal flow. To that extent, a borrower's ability to become an expert in private lending—and in doing it safely for all parties involved—can set them apart from other borrowers who are also seeking capital partners.

Additionally, private lending can benefit active investors by keeping cash working for them in between projects. We often have investors ask us to place their funds temporarily in a short-term (six to ten month) loan while they search for their next project.

The (Re)tired Investor

If you do not want to fix toilets or deal with tenant evictions, we don't blame you! There are many investors who are busy W-2 income earners, stay-at-home parents with young families, or who simply do not have the desire or propensity to become active real estate investors and prefer the idea of diversifying in real estate through private lending. Sometimes being the lender can be a lot less stressful than owning and managing the property.

Additionally, many seasoned landlords transition into private lending when they are at a chapter in life where they are entering retirement and looking to simplify their lifestyle as well as their estate planning by liquidating their rental portfolio so that the properties do not become a burden to themselves or to their beneficiaries. Private lending provides these types of investors with more time to enjoy their retirement as well as a strong source of passive cash flow without the extra hassles associated with rental property management.

The Newbie Investor

If you are a new or aspiring real estate investor, chances are you started out on BiggerPockets and at local real estate investing meetups learning anything and everything you could about how to get started in real estate investing. With a limited amount of capital but an unlimited amount of devotion and desire to learn, you quickly realized that activities like wholesaling—despite not needing a ton of cash to start out with—isn't the right path for you, and that flipping either required more money than you had or a partnership you weren't yet comfortable initiating with complete strangers.

But what do you do next with only a seemingly small amount of capital to start out with? Private lending can help you passively grow your capital to a sizeable amount so that you can eventually start actively investing. Some grow to like the passive-income approach so much that they abandon previous plans to go into active investing and remain private lenders indefinitely.

The Private-Placement Fund Participant

Understanding the core concepts of private lending can help you choose the right fund to invest in. Plus, it's critical to know what key questions to ask a fund manager before choosing to place your capital with them. While we won't dive too deep into how to choose the right fund to invest in, we will explore the pros and cons associated with either doing it yourself or going with a more passive and supported approach like a pooled mortgage fund. Hopefully this book will shed light on which path those of you contemplating private lending as an investment tool should choose, and why it's a better choice for you and your desired lifestyle.

In this book, we'll address the entire process through the lens of a lender, but the concepts and processes outlined will be universally beneficial no matter which side of the transaction you happen to be on. An educated investor with realistic expectations and knowledge of safeguards makes any investment safer!

HOW TO READ THIS BOOK

Getting started in private lending can be an overwhelming process, especially if you are going it alone. There are so many components and considerations to think about and endless ways to creatively structure the loan terms to fit both the borrower's needs and your own. We liken the private lending process to solving a 1000-piece puzzle, where each piece looks similar at first glance, but when you study two pieces side by side, you start to see a lot of differences in the coloring, the edges, and where and how they might fit into the overall picture. Even if you were to put the entire puzzle together again, it would be equally as challenging to repeat the process. The subtle nuances of each puzzle piece can make it difficult to create muscle memory so the process is easier the next time around.

But never fear! We have developed a systematic approach to help you learn all the necessary steps of the entire loan life cycle. It starts when you begin looking for a new loan to fund and ends when your loan is finally paid off in full. We walk you through the entire process with a repeatable set of steps that can help you do it all over again. We call this system "C.P.R. lending," and it will help you manage each step in the loan life cycle from beginning to end. The C.P.R. lending system breaks out the stages of the loan process, the considerations to make in each stage, and the risks and rewards of each stage to help guide your decision-making.

The C.P.R. Lending™ System
Your Lifeline to Private Lending

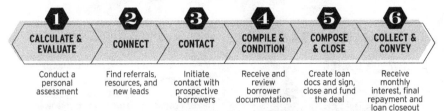

① CALCULATE & EVALUATE	② CONNECT	③ CONTACT	④ COMPILE & CONDITION	⑤ COMPOSE & CLOSE	⑥ COLLECT & CONVEY
Conduct a personal assessment	Find referrals, resources, and new leads	Initiate contact with prospective borrowers	Receive and review borrower documentation	Create loan docs and sign, close and fund the deal	Receive monthly interest, final repayment and loan closeout

PEOPLE. PROPERTY. PAPERWORK.

Every step in the C.P.R. lending process will cover WHO to involve, WHAT to consider related to the property and project, and HOW to collect or create the appropriate paperwork needed to safely pass each step.

RISKS AND REWARDS.

When faced with a multitude of different ways to lend private capital, you will learn how to identify your personal risks and limitations as well as potential rewards associated with lending under certain terms and circumstances at each step of the loan life cycle.

C'ing the Big Picture

The "C" in C.P.R. lending covers each stage of the loan cycle. Each chapter represents its own "C." We designed the book this way so that you could return to any chapter and reread it when you are in that stage of the loan. This will allow you to quickly and easily reference something in the future. It is kind of like the children's book series Choose Your Own Adventure, where you (as the reader) decide what happens next and skip around the book based on those choices. Similarly, we've designed this book to walk you through the storyline of a private loan, but you can also skip around as you see fit, based on what you want to learn about and do next. Someone has presented you with a loan opportunity, but you don't know what to do first? Skip to Chapter Five: "Contact." The title report is back but it is full of special exceptions and you don't know what to do next? Go directly to Chapter Eleven: "Underwriting Deep Dive—Paperwork."

The Steps of the Loan Life Cycle (the C's) We Will Be Discussing:

STEP 1	CALCULATE & EVALUATE	Establish personal risks and lending criteria
STEP 2	CONNECT	Make connections to find potential borrowers and vendors
STEP 3	CONTACT	Initiate contact with prospective borrowers and vendors
STEP 4	COMPILE & CONDITION	Receive and review borrower documentation
STEP 5	COMPOSE & CLOSE	Create loan documents and manage the loan closing process
STEP 6	COLLECT & CONVEY	Receive monthly interest, final repayment, and loan closeout

Minding Your P's and R's

Within each "C", which represents a stage in the loan life cycle, we will also cover three P's. Think of the P's as fact-finding missions. The three P's are: Person, Property, and Paperwork. The first two P's tell you what people and what property and project considerations are involved in that part of the loan cycle. The last P covers what paperwork is involved in that stage of the loan. This includes both the paperwork you need to request as the lender and paperwork you need to generate as the lender.

PERSON	In each step of the C.P.R. lending system, you will learn who the key players are and who is responsible for the key outcomes of that step. While the borrower is always front and center, there are also other individuals who help collect data, process paperwork, and validate certain aspects of the property or paperwork.
PROPERTY	The collateral being used to secure your loan will be the property. Often that property is going to be renovated, so it is also important to understand the project scope and financials.
PAPERWORK	Private lending has different paperwork to either request, review, create, sign, or provide. We'll let you know what paperwork is required for each step in the C.P.R. lending process.

Lastly, each stage of the loan cycle has specific and unique considerations for Risk and Reward. We will cover how to balance your risk tolerance with your potential reward. These can be very specific to you as an individual, but we will touch on some broad areas of consideration. Everyone has different risk tolerances, so don't think of it as doing something "right" or "wrong" but rather as doing what's best for you and your comfort level. Of course, evaluating the rewards is also a part of the process. Knowing what could go wrong is just half of the equation, but you also need to know what could go right. After all, this book is designed to give you information about private lending and how to do it more safely.

At the end of the day, these will be your personal processes and preferences to define. Since the concept and practice of private lending is so widely varied, we can only give you the general factors to contemplate. You alone will be responsible for determining what you can and cannot live with in regard to lending out your own money and managing those trade-offs accordingly. Hopefully, this will help you recognize your no-go areas before funding a loan so you don't get into a sticky situation after your money is lent out.

Keep It Simple, Stupid!

We are not calling you stupid, but we certainly felt a little dense when we were new private lenders. A few things we found overwhelming when starting out in private lending were the overly engineered processes and complicated jargon used throughout the industry. At our first private lender conference, we remember sitting among a sea of mostly men in suits listening to them talk about capital markets and how many assets they had under management (the amount of capital they used to lend out). Sometimes they would ask us what asset classes we specialized in (in lay terms, it's just property types). Meanwhile, we sat there with shocked looks on our faces like a pair of deer in headlights. It was intimidating, to say the least!

After years of being in the industry, we found it's not as difficult as it was made out to be, but it will take time and experience to learn all the ins and outs. While a certain language needs to be used within the alternative-lending industry as a whole, you don't need to get caught up in it as a truly private, individual lender. Sure, you may need to speak the same language if you are looking to scale your lending into a full-time practice, but that's not what this book is about. It's about getting started and using private lending as a passive income source. And—from what we've noticed over time—borrowers tend to appreciate the fact that we keep it simple and accessible by speaking in a language everyone can understand.

In this book, we put private lending into easy-to-understand terminology and overly simplified steps. It is very easy to get caught up in the specific language of real estate and lending. While knowing those words can be helpful when communicating with potential borrowers or even other lenders, we wanted to make this process easy to digest and provide real-world stories and examples, which help drive home key concepts.

Additionally, we have organized this book in two parts. First, we will introduce the stages involved in privately funding a loan, which will provide you with a complete look at the loan life cycle from start to finish. This will include the key objective and a high-level overview of the tasks involved in each step. In the second part, we will go deeper into how to evaluate and process a loan request to ensure it meets your basic lending standards. This is also known as underwriting a loan. Here, we will cover what essential documents to review and what key metrics or datapoints to assess, and how these impact the overall risk of the loan.

The intent here is to provide a baseline understanding of the process before diving into the details of how it's done. Think of private lending like learning how to fish. First, you have to learn how the entire process works, including how to bait the hook, how to find a location suitable to catching fish, and how to identify key indicators that fish will be present. Only then will you learn how to cast your line and, hopefully, reel in a big one. The "art" of fishing requires figuring out where to look for a good fishing hole. Similar to underwriting, there are a lot of key factors that come into play, including asking local experts, looking for other fishermen gathered in the same spot, and observing common signs like fish jumping out of the water.

We also have provided bonus materials and resources that you may need to use along the way. You can find these at www.biggerpockets.com/lendingbonus. It is unreasonable to think we can cover every option related to handling a particular task or reviewing a specific document in a single book. Much of your learning will come through personal experience. These downloadable materials will help you when certain circumstances do come your way that were not completely covered in this entry-level introduction to private lending.

Chapter 2
THE BASICS

More than likely you've picked up this book because you've heard, read, or talked about private money lending in some form or fashion, and it piqued your interest to learn more. Maybe you've learned enough to be dangerous, or maybe you just heard someone discuss the general concept of private lending and the only thing you recall is the generous rates of return. Either way, you obviously felt compelled enough to take matters into your own hands, literally, with this book.

Regardless of where you are in your investment journey, we are first going to talk about the overall process so you can get a basic understanding of what private lending means in the context of this book. We begin by laying the foundation for real estate financing and private lending. Once you have those fundamental concepts down, we dive into the actual steps to funding a private money loan. But don't think this is going to be a linear process because it likely won't. For those of you who are sequential learners, this will probably drive you nuts, but bear with us. Take your time to digest these concepts, be comfortable with starting and stopping the process, and accept that you will probably make mistakes along the way. Remember: Private lending can be very collaborative, so reach out and ask questions of other lenders and attorneys familiar with lending in your desired market. Doing so will allow you to learn from the smaller mistakes rather than the big ones. Get the basics, involve the right people, and it will be smooth sailing.

WHAT IS PRIVATE LENDING?

While private lending can take a lot of forms, this book is going to focus on lending to people who are buying preexisting single-family homes and small multifamily dwellings like duplexes. For simplicity we're going to begin with a common lending scenario of a borrower who needs funding to fix-and-flip a residential property for profit. Once you are comfortable after a few loans, you can then pursue more specialized lending. This simplified look at private lending allows a beginner to understand the investment, learn the asset inside and out, and then make an informed decision.

Many of you may have purchased single-family homes, so the leap into this type of real estate investing and lending won't be as far of a stretch as it would be to start lending on commercial property types such as retail, office space, etc. We do want to point out one key difference between financing a property for your home and financing an investment property. The traditional home-buying process typically requires the borrower to get pre-qualified with a mortgage professional—this helps the buyers know how much they are qualified to purchase. However, in real estate investing, a subject property typically needs to be identified because the loan is underwritten mostly by the asset (the property) and not borrower credit or financials.

Beginning your private lending journey with a type of property you know well, such as residential homes, is the easiest way to transition into real estate investing. Plus, with this style of private lending, you will never be short on potential borrowers or projects to lend on. The opportunities to lend on homes and small multifamily property assets are plentiful.

The "Vanilla" First Loan

The basics of private lending are simple: You have money to lend out to someone who will put that money to work for you. The loan will be secured by real estate. At some agreed-upon future date, the borrower will repay your capital with interest.

For the purposes of this book, and as a recommendation from us on where to start your lending if you have little to no experience in real estate, we will use the following "vanilla" loan example throughout the book for context:
- **Property type:** Detached, single-family house (not a townhome or condominium with shared walls)
- **Property condition:** In need of cosmetic repairs such as new paint, floors, kitchens, and bathrooms (not major renovation needs like structural issues or an addition)
- **Project strategy:** Borrower plans to fix-and-flip (rehab and put property back on the market) or will BRRRR (buy, rehab, rent, refinance, repeat) out of the private loan

Why Private Lending?

You may ask why private lending is so advantageous. You may even have the impression that it's risky. You see the infomercials and the flashy covers of books and magazines about buying ugly houses and fixing them to sell for a profit. You hear horror stories of landlords getting their homes trashed by terrible tenants. Those are the most common first impressions of real estate investing. However, what no one will bother to tell new investors is there are so many other ways to invest in real estate. The world of investment is a big place, and real estate investing encompasses so many different paths to wealth that limiting the focus to just fix-and-flips or buying rentals is a mistake. Private lending allows you as a lender to essentially act like a bank. Within limitations of the laws (which we will talk about later), you have the ability to dictate the loan terms, including interest rates, fees, repayment schedules, the types of properties, how much you are willing to lend, and so much more.

Remember, as the lender, you're not responsible for taking care of the property! If a toilet breaks on a Sunday afternoon, no one will call you. If a contractor doesn't show up for the third day in a row to work on the floors, you won't be the one chasing them down to find out what is going on. There is rarely a last-minute emergency that needs to be handled immediately in private lending. Those tasks all belong to the person we call the "active investor." Private lending falls into the category of "passive investing" in real estate.

If you ask about the difference between active and passive investing, you'll find a variety of definitions available to you. For us, passive investing means you get the choice to be as involved in that investment as you want and when you want. Active investing requires your constant attention, and if you step away, the investment often lags or fails to perform. Passive investing doesn't mean you won't do anything. It means there's often a lighter workload, or the work is done at the beginning of the opportunity. Once the capital is deployed, it's merely a matter of receiving updates and regular payments, if that was negotiated in the transaction.

Benefits of Private Lending for the Active Investor

It's a common misconception that borrowers who need private lending have poor credit or cannot get conventional lending from a bank or financial institution. While this may be the case with some borrowers, the need for private financing goes beyond creditworthiness and extends to those involved in real estate investing who need money fast—faster than banks and conventional lending can accommodate. The need to buy properties quickly, without hassle, is the primary reason most borrowers are willing to pay higher interest rates from a private lender. Here are a few reasons why active investors may pursue private lending.

- The property doesn't qualify for conventional financing due to its current distressed or unlivable condition.
- The borrower wants to present an attractive offer with a quick closing (often fewer than twenty-one days).
- The borrower is looking for simplified underwriting practices, which could include no third-party appraisals, no income verification, and little to no credit requirements.
- The borrower's debt-to-income ratio is too high to qualify for a conventional loan.
- The borrower is self-employed and has difficulties qualifying for conventional financing.

FINANCING FUNDAMENTALS

Next, let's discuss some basic concepts of lending. For those of you with some experience in lending or real estate investing, this may serve as a refresher for you. For those who are beginners, these general financing terms provide a necessary foundation so you can understand the private lending process more fully and not get lost or overwhelmed along the way.

First, you need to know the various ways to lend money to a borrower. These are not mutually exclusive and can be a combination of each category below.

Consumer vs. Commercial

Consumer lending involves a loan that will be used for personal use, such as buying a house to move into as your primary home. It could also be a credit card you have in your own name or a loan you secure to purchase a new car or RV. Conversely, commercial loans, also known as business-purpose loans, are those used for business or investment intentions. An example of a commercial loan opportunity would be a real estate investor buying a house as a flip project or to turn into a rental. In this book, we want to remain in the business-purpose loan area as much as possible, as it provides the best returns, potentially reduces exposure to usury and other consumer-protection requirements, and targets a large audience such as real estate investors. We will explore in more detail what constitutes a business-purpose loan later in the book, but it is important to understand a general definition of it early on.

Secured vs. Unsecured

Loans can be secured by collateral, or they can be unsecured, meaning there is no collateral safeguarding the loan. Collateral can be in the form of real property (real estate), personal property (vehicle, equipment, or anything with value), or a business's assets. On the flip side, unsecured loans are those without any collateral, such as revolving lines of credit (credit cards). The latter are typically underwritten by the borrower's credit score and history. We recommend that you make all your private loans secured by real property with sufficient equity protection. Again, more on that later!

Mortgage vs. Deed of Trust

When real property is put up as collateral to secure a loan, a lien is placed against it and recorded in public records. Depending on the state in which you reside, this could be recorded at the county clerk's office or the city recorder's office. Liens are recorded in one of two ways: mortgages or deeds of trust. We have included a list of which states use mortgages and which use deeds of trust in the resource area of this book. Use this as a general framework, but do not use it as a replacement for legal advice from a qualified attorney.

Recourse vs. Nonrecourse

You may have heard of nonrecourse and recourse debt. Nonrecourse debt means that someone is not personally and individually responsible for the money a business entity takes on as debt. Nonrecourse debt is generally for businesses that have either a long history of operating profitably or some assets to use as collateral for the loan. Recourse debt means that the individual owner(s) of the business are personally responsible for the money owed should the business fail to pay its obligations or goes out of business. Usually, debt instruments like credit cards or home equity lines of credit (HELOCs) are forms of recourse debt, meaning the owner has agreed that they are personally responsible to cover this debt. We recommend all your loans be recourse loans so that your borrower is personally tied to the loan you fund.

Here's a chart that explains the various types of common loans available in the financing world and how they are categorized using the terms we identified above.

	UNSECURED	SECURED
BUSINESS	Small Business Administration (SBA) loans Warehouse lines of credit (LOCs)	Rental or investment property loans Fix-and-flips Equipment loans Heavy-machinery loans
PERSONAL	Student loans Payday loans Revolving LOCs (credit cards)	Auto loans RV loans Primary-home loans Second homes/vacation-home loans/home equity loans (HELs)/home equity line of credit (HELOC) using primary home

Conventional Lending vs. Alternative Lending

Conventional lending, for the purposes of this book, will be oversimplified to be any loan a borrower can get through a financial institution, such as a bank or a mortgage broker. While conventional lending will offer the lowest rates and have strict lending guidelines imposed by government agencies such as Fannie Mae and Freddie Mac, the steep underwriting associated with conventional lending is for consumer protection. It's an effective way to ensure borrowers do not get into a loan they cannot afford, but it can be a cumbersome system for real estate investors.

Because of the strict overlays, many real estate investors turn to alternative lending options. These include hard money, private money, and other alternative lending solutions such as non-QM, or non-qualified mortgages.

Hard Money vs. Private Money

Hard money is traditionally meant to describe using a hard asset as collateral to secure a loan. Hard-money lenders are financial service companies that specialize in asset-based loans used for business or commercial purposes. While a married couple could not use hard money to buy their first home, a real estate investor benefits from having financial solutions without the consumer-protection overlays associated with conventional lending. For both private and hard money, the underwriting analysis often focuses heavily on the property, while the traditional bank loan focuses on the borrower.

The difference between hard-money lenders and private lenders can be summed up in a few ways. One key difference is the hard-money lender actively runs a lending business and likely has a strong presence in their market. Meanwhile, a private lender is usually an individual or a small group of partners who lend out their own money and perhaps some capital from people within their personal network. This seemingly secret society of private lenders may not lend full-time and may have other "day" jobs; they can therefore be difficult to source as an active investor. In fact, there are books written about how to raise capital as an active real estate investor from private sources! (See *Raising Private Capital* by Matt Faircloth.) Additionally, source of capital is a key difference between hard money and private money. Private capital is not associated with an institution, bank, or corporation.

There has been a push in recent years to rebrand the hard-money space as private lending. This is due, in part, to the negative connotations associated with hard-money lending in the past. This can be confusing, as it blurs the line between hard-money lenders and truly private lenders like you and me. We like to keep the distinction between an individual private lender (or a small partnership of private lenders) and the "big dogs" within the hard-money lending world who have seemingly endless access to capital, corporate counsel, and complex capital deployment strategies. If you fall in love with private lending and make the decision to scale your practice into a more actively managed business, you may need to learn additional concepts, add human resources, research other capital sources, or define a capital deployment strategy for yourself. But for now, we recommend sticking to the basics.

	HARD MONEY	PRIVATE MONEY
TYPE OF INVESTING	Active business	Passive business
BRAND/MARKET PRESENCE	Typically has company branding and presence in the market	May use personal name or an LLC to lend out, with no major branding or market presence
SOURCE OF CAPITAL	Can use a pooled mortgage fund, or warehouse line of credit; might be backed by venture capital, hedge funds, or other institutional capital sources	Can be funds from a private individual, a self-directed retirement account, capital from friends, family, or others within their network, or a pooled mortgage fund
LOAN VOLUME	Annual volume is typically in the millions of dollars	Annual volume is dependent on how much capital is available to lend by the individual
LENDING LIMITATIONS	May have strict lending guidelines associated with the capital source	Restrictions are their own personal guidelines

KEY COMPONENTS TO A LOAN

A loan has many different aspects to it. You will need to understand these components to not only set your own lending criteria but also to aid in the process of qualifying and underwriting a loan. Here are a few terms you will need to know:

Principal Loan Amount

This is the principal amount of money to be borrowed.

Example: You lend out $100,000. That's the principal loan amount.

Interest Rate

The interest rate is represented as a percentage of the principal loan amount that will be a monthly cost for the borrower. This is also expressed as your expected rate of return on your investment.

Example: You lend out your $100,000 at 12 percent annually. The 12 percent is your interest rate.

Monthly Payment

This can be either an interest-only payment or a principal and interest payment that would require the borrower to pay down the principal loan amount each month. While you can negotiate a different frequency of payment, monthly is most common.

Example: If you have an interest rate of 12 percent on your $100,000 loan and it's an interest-only loan, then the monthly payment will be $1,000 ($12,000 divided by 12 months).

Loan-to-Value

Also known as LTV, this is a ratio between the loan amount and the value of the property. The lower the loan-to-value, the more equity there is in the property and, therefore, the lower the risk.

Example: If you lend $100,000 on a property worth $150,000, the loan-to-value is 66 percent. You get this by dividing $100,000 by $150,000.

Origination Points

Points are another way of describing the percentage of the loan that will be charged as costs of originating the loan for the borrower. Origination points can be paid at any point during the loan, but they are traditionally paid when your borrower closes on the purchase of the property you are lending on.

Example: If you charge two points for your loan origination of a $100,000 loan, you are charging 2 percent of the principal loan amount of $100,000, or $2,000 in loan origination fees.

Term of Loan

This refers to the length of time the loan is being held by the borrower, and any extensions that may be written into your promissory note. Many private lenders prefer shorter loan terms—think months, not years. Typical private money loans range from three months to two years. The length of the loan is determined by you as the lender. Some prefer to have long loan terms because they do not want to deal with underwriting a loan every few months, whereas other lenders like the "churn" of new loans to collect more origination points.

> *Example:* The $100,000 loan will be due twelve months after the borrower closes on the property to buy it. If you have monthly payments and a 12 percent annual rate, that means the borrower will be paying the lender (you) $1,000 every month for up to twelve months before the borrower repays the full amount at the end of the twelfth month.

There are more terms and components you will need to become familiar with as part of the private lending process, but this is a good baseline of lending knowledge to start with. Now that you understand a little more about the general concepts of financing loans and private lending, let's get started with the good stuff—C.P.R lending, your lifeline to becoming a private lender.

BEFORE JUMPING INTO PRIVATE LENDING

Private lending is a highly nuanced industry, and mistakes are inevitable. The act of funding a private loan is full of so many variables—some you can control but many you cannot—that it can be difficult for a newcomer to develop any sort of muscle memory. Each borrower's profile and loan purpose are uniquely different, which makes the evaluation of person, property, and paperwork a complicated process. No two borrowers are the same. No two deals are the same. No two properties are the same. So get used to the idea that you will probably miss something or make a miscalculation. Get others involved early and often, and pay to have legal documents drawn up to further cover yourself. Get input from lenders who may be more experienced, but be prepared to get a different answer from each lender.

Even the most seasoned of private lenders have made errors in judgment, miscalculations, and omissions—plenty of small ones and perhaps a few big ones that may have left an emotional or financial scar or two. The goal after reading this book will be to screw up *before* the consequences are too steep and, most importantly, to identify the red flags so it doesn't happen again. But mishaps *will* happen and if this alone makes you queasy, you might not yet be ready for the journey, because there is no room for perfection in private lending. Even if you have mastered the art of private lending, there are still variables outside your control which can adversely affect the performance of your loan. Just think what would happen if your borrower were suddenly hit by a bus midway through the renovations of a property! Not that we want this to happen, but it's advisable to plan for worst-case scenarios.

We certainly are not trying to be alarmists but it's worth the effort to say up front that private lending comes with inherent risks. And those risks are greater when you are first starting out. For those of you who picked up this book expecting to read an instructional textbook, we want to emphasize that this is more contemplation than calculation. This book is more about shaping a mindset than relaying a method. There tends to be more art than science in lending, and the art only improves with practice. We will teach you a methodology that is predictable in theory and yet so free-form in application. While we present the content within a systems framework, there is a lot of critical thinking and intro-spection involved on your part. There can be variables due to not only personal preferences and risk tolerances, but also factors such as market conditions, where you are in an economic market cycle, the lending laws in your chosen market, and the business model you choose to pursue as a private lender. The road map is so individualized because we don't know where the end goal is located, much less where you are starting from. Just take one step at a time and ask for help along the way.

Chapter 3
CALCULATE & EVALUATE

| CALCULATE & EVALUATE | CONNECT | CONTACT | COMPILE & CONDITION | COMPOSE & CLOSE | COLLECT & CONVEY |

CALCULATE & EVALUATE QUICK PEEK

C	**CALCULATE & EVALUATE** In this pre-step, you will conduct a pre-assessment of your investment needs and the reasons behind why you want to get started in private lending.		
P	**PERSON** You as the lender will be evaluating capital availability, risk tolerances, and considerations for timelines.	**PROPERTY** You will evaluate what types of properties you are willing to lend on and where.	**PAPERWORK** You will complete a Personal Private Lender Assessment to explore your private lending needs, wants, and desires.
R	**RISKS AND REWARDS** Not completing this step thoroughly or at all could put you in some tough situations later down the line. If not done or not done well, you could have emotional, financial, or logistical consequences.		

This pre-step on your private lending journey will look at the amount of money you are ready to invest and evaluate *how* you want to lend this money. We call this Calculate & Evaluate. You will also define *why* you are getting into private lending in the first place. Your "why" will serve as a beacon as you navigate your private lending priorities.

Most private lenders we talk to recount similar stories. They successfully do a handful of loans only for the floodgates to open with a flurry of loan requests and prospective borrowers suddenly appearing overnight. We, too, experienced this surge in demand. It's not an uncommon situation for private lenders like yourself to become quickly overwhelmed with an abundance of lending opportunities. Defining your "why" up front will help you make better decisions based on how you see private lending fitting into your desired lifestyle and how you hope to evolve over time, if at all.

If you truly cherish your freedom of time and want to be a parent first—and an investor second—then it is important to set limits up front about how much private lending volume you want to take on and whether your intentions are to scale or to stay small and passive. Alternatively, maybe you desire to create an active private lending business for yourself to establish a source of generational wealth for your family. Regardless of what your values and priorities are, identifying them before you begin lending will steer you in the right direction so you don't get in over your head. Determining how private lending will fit into your everyday life is a very important step that every aspiring private lender should complete. You only need to do it once, which is why we consider it a pre-step. However, you will want to revisit these goals and your "why" over time as your lifestyle needs change with various life events such as kids, career moves, and retirement.

This pre-step will involve two parts.

1. Complete a Personal Private Lender Assessment to define your investing needs and wants, desired outcomes, and overall reasons for wanting to get started in private lending.
2. Review standard private lending loan terms and start the process to define your lending guidelines in rates, fees, and terms.

PERSON

The most important person in this stage of lending is you, the lender. Private lending can be tailored to suit any sort of investor and can often meet a wide variety of needs. Most people say they want some level of financial independence or they want to leave their W-2 job because they can't stand some aspect of it. You may feel the same way. But what you *really* want is the ability to do what you want, when you want, and where you want. That's ultimately at the heart of most people's desires for financial independence.

Private lending provides the flexibility of being an investor without the burden of being tied to your phone all day looking for deals, talking to distressed sellers, meeting contractors, or screening tenants. You don't even have to be in the same country as the property! We certainly know many active real estate investors who manage their investments from afar—whether that is flipping, overseeing rentals, or repositioning a property—but it can take years to put the proper systems in place. With private lending, you can go remote on your very first deal. If you have electricity, internet access, and phone service, you can do private lending from anywhere in the world.

If this doesn't sound appealing, please give this book to someone who may find that lifestyle valuable. Otherwise, keep reading!

Personal Risk Tolerance

The biggest worry in private lending (or any lending, for that matter) is "Will I be repaid?" The reason we are doing all this due diligence on the borrower, the property, the loan terms, and the signing disclosures and paperwork is to solve that one question. What we do to further mitigate our risk as lenders can be very individual in nature, but the goal is the same: lower the risk of losing our money, then evaluate the return on the investment. Make it safer, then worry about the return.

Calculating your personal risk tolerance and reasons for private lending are of utmost importance here. This will shape your business model, where you lend, who you lend to, how you lend, what type of property you are willing to lend on, and so many more details. It would be unfair of us to present to you a defined list of criteria because we do not know how you operate, what your goals are, and how risk adverse you may be in your investments.

Remember earlier when we told you we once had a prospective capital investor tell us as soon as we met him that he "didn't get out bed for anything less than 13 percent"? It took us a little by surprise because we had mostly worked with investors who preferred a little lower return in exchange for less risk. The bottom line here is you need to determine for yourself, and perhaps any potentially affected individuals such as a spouse, what that risk threshold might look like. To help you in your self-discovery, we will cover different factors you will need to address before moving on to the next step.

Goals and Lifestyle Considerations

Why do you want to invest in the first place? Avoid the typical "I want financial freedom" answer. Everyone wants that, but what does that specifically look like to you and why is that important? How will your life change? Who will be in your life? What are you doing once you are financially independent? Are you even striving for financial independence? Take a moment to really think. We encourage you to sit and write down your answers. Private lending is just one of many ways you could earn additional income, and it doesn't have to be the only way you choose to do so.

Knowledge and Skills (and Desires)

Now that you have an idea of why you are taking these first steps, let's evaluate what your strengths and areas of growth are, in addition to your risk tolerance. There are several ways to issue a loan that are only partially guided by the laws of the state. In many ways, private lending is a collaborative endeavor, since the terms of the loan can be largely dictated by you as the lender in conjunction with the needs of the borrower. Establishing which criteria are nonnegotiable will help guide you when you are reaching out to potential borrowers and evaluating lending opportunities.

What you want to do is figure out what your ideal loan looks like, at least in theory. You may not know every variable of lending, but it is important to have an idea of what type of property you would want to lend on, who your ideal borrower might be, and what loan terms you want to make it worth the risk of lending. No investment is without risk, and private lending is not immune from that.

Even if an "expert" provides you with an opinion, this person is not responsible for your investment choices, nor are they the one holding any of the risk. Therefore, it's incumbent upon you to define your own criteria and evaluate the risks versus the rewards. In the Paperwork part of this pre-step you'll assess your strengths and the places where you may need assistance from an outside resource. While you might be skilled at a certain task, you may simply decide you do not have enough time or inclination to take on that responsibility. That is completely fine. Outlining your needs, wants, and hard nos in advance will be useful in procuring the right support in your network.

Outside of lending expertise, it's important to state up front that private lending does require a reasonable amount of understanding about real estate investing in general. While you may not need to know everything there is to know about flipping, having a baseline awareness will aid you in your due diligence on loans. After all, the deal analysis that flippers conduct is very similar to and uses the same metrics as the evaluations lenders use for the deal too. We therefore encourage you to figure out what you do not know about real estate investing, particularly house flipping since that is where we will be centering most of our lending conversations. This is one of the most popular and, quite frankly, "vanilla" private loans that a lender could do. You can research and learn more on websites such as Bigger Pockets.com, where you have access to webinars, books, podcasts, and a very active online forum dedicated to all topics of real estate investing.

PROPERTY

As mentioned previously, there are many ways to structure and fund a private loan. One aspect of the loan that is purely subjective to the lender's preference and comfort level would be which types of properties and projects to lend on. We recommend that new and novice lenders with little to no experience focus on loans associated with residential properties, such as detached single-family or small multifamily properties. However, if you are an experienced commercial real estate broker looking to get into private lending, perhaps you would feel most comfortable taking on your first loans using commercial property types instead. It's completely up to you, but in the Calculate & Evaluate stage, you should contemplate what property types you are comfortable with.

Typical Property Types
- Single-family houses
- Multifamily (two to four units)
- Commercial multifamily (five or more units)
- Commercial buildings (mixed use, retail, office, hospitality, etc.)
- Construction/development projects
- Condominiums, townhouses, manufactured homes, mobile homes
- Self-storage, mobile home parks, industrial
- Land

Other considerations and personal preferences related to the property include:
- What type of property or properties would you be comfortable owning if you had to foreclose on a property?
- Are there any particular aspects of a property that would make you not want to own it? (Think unusual construction like container homes; proximity to highways, major roads, airports, or railways; or presence of a septic

tank in an area where most of the homes have municipal sewer service.)
- What area or market would you be comfortable owning a property in?
- What is the maximum loan-to-value you would be comfortable lending?
- What types of projects would you be comfortable lending on? (We suggest keeping things simple early on and only lending on move in–ready homes or those requiring minimal renovation, also known as a cosmetic rehab.)

Don't worry if you cannot answer all of these questions right now. We simply want to outline the key questions you should answer over time. After you have completed this book, you will have additional foundational knowledge to answer a few more questions, and after you've completed a loan or two, you may want to revisit your responses and change some of your answers. The assessment will become more fluid as you gain more knowledge and experience as a lender.

PAPERWORK

In the Calculate & Evaluate pre-step, the primary piece of paperwork you will need is the Personal Private Lender Assessment, which can be found in the supplemental materials at www.biggerpockets.com/lendingbonus. Completing this assessment will give you a head start in establishing lending guidelines for yourself. Think about these questions and write down the answers. There is a lot to learn but coming back to these fundamentals will help you in times of indecision.

Financial Foundation
1. How much money do you have to invest?
2. How much money do you plan to keep in reserves for household or personal emergencies?
3. What sources of capital do you plan to use for private lending?
   - Savings
   - Self-directed retirement plans
   - Family trust
   - HELOC or other borrowed capital
   - Pooled funds from a handful of family/friends/colleagues
   - Other: _____
4. What is the estimated amount of capital you will have to start lending? (You may not want to use all of the money you have to invest into one type of investment.)

a. Will you be relying on the monthly income to sustain your quality of life, or will you be saving this additional income for a future date?
b. Will this be a diversification strategy for your investment portfolio?
c. Will this be a primary source of income for your household?
d. Are you looking at this as a supplemental passive source of income only?

Motivations and Expectations
1. Why do you want to start private lending?
2. What are you seeking for expected returns on your investment? What range of interest rates or monthly interest income would you like to achieve?
3. What personal, family, and other non-monetary reasons do you have for private lending?
4. What goals do you have for your private lending investments? (e.g., build a business, establish a side hustle, put some excess money to work)
5. Do you ultimately want to build this into a small business that involves capital raising from other sources outside your current network?

Time Commitment and Experience
1. How active do you want to be in your private lending investments?
2. How much experience do you have in real estate investing?
3. How much time do you realistically have to devote to private lending activities?
   a. On a daily basis?
   b. On a weekly basis?
   c. On a monthly basis?

Lending Preferences
1. Would you prefer to originate new loans, buy existing loans that borrowers are paying on, or purchase discount loans where the borrower is behind on payments? (While this book covers originating new loans, these latter two ways of investing in real estate in the mortgage space also exist.)
2. How much are you comfortable lending in any one project (total dollar amount)?
3. What loan-to-value (amount of the loan compared to the value of the property) would you be comfortable with? (A typical range is 60 percent to 75 percent for new or more conservative lenders.)
4. With what frequency would you like interest payments to be made?

5. Do you want to collect interest payments and provide a payoff letter to borrowers? (Hint: You don't have to do this yourself; there are companies that will do it for you.)

Strengths and Opportunities for Growth

Now that you have evaluated your "why" and a bit of *how* you want to participate in private lending, let's look at your strengths and the skills you already have as well as your overall risk tolerance.

Personal Strengths and Growth Areas
- What skills do you feel you excel at naturally?
- What skills or knowledge do you need to build or find help with?
- What resources do you think you may need to complete a loan transaction?

Personal Comfort Level with Private Lending
- How do you feel about lending out money in general?
- How comfortable are you with a loan payment being late?
- How comfortable would you be with seeking legal recourse as soon as a loan payment is late?
- How would you feel if a loan payment was more than thirty days late but fewer than sixty days late?
- How would you feel contacting a borrower directly to see if a payment could be made?

RISKS AND REWARDS

An attractive reward to private lending is the rate of return. Generally, interest rates increase with the level of perceived risk in an investment. Private lending offers returns ranging from 8 percent to 14 percent on an annual basis, depending on your market, borrower experience, and other terms you may offer in the loan. The reward is the interest payments coming to you each month. This income is often a primary reason many investors want to pursue private lending. While private lending may be considered more passive than more traditional versions of real estate investing, there are still some actions you will need to take. Nothing really is truly 100 percent passive. Everything is going to require some action on your part.

Like any other investment, private lending carries some risk. You need to consider the return *of* capital before the return *on* capital. The main question you want to answer in this entire loan process is how safe the capital is in this lending opportunity. The major risk is default by the borrower and the length of time it may take to get your full principal and interest owed to you. Fortunately, several safeguards can be built into the loan that allow the lender to foreclose on the property and sell it at public auction to recoup your capital or to have the borrower pay the loan in a timely manner as agreed.

You also may not know the condition of the property at the time you get the title. This is another reason to involve an attorney early in the lending process. You will want to know the local laws regulating foreclosure, how long it takes, and what could slow it down. Think of this as risk-mitigation strategy No. 1. "Hope for the best and plan for the worst" is a great way to approach private lending.

Another risk in private lending is the opportunity cost of doing a loan. Real estate tends to be an illiquid investment, as we discussed before. Your capital could be tied up for a year or longer. That means you won't be able to take advantage of other opportunities that may come along during that time. This could be anything from starting a business, loaning on another project, or even deciding to buy some investment property yourself. In some rare cases, there may be buyers for your loan if you truly need the capital back, but they are unlikely to pay full price for your loan, so you stand to lose some of the capital you put into it. Do not depend on having that money back in your bank account should something go wrong in your life or if you want to pursue another investment opportunity. Just as the borrower signed on the dotted line for the loan terms, you agreed to those loan terms as well. Only lend out what makes you feel comfortable, and know that you won't have access to it for a specific amount of time or even longer than original loan terms stipulate if the borrower defaults on the loan. Keep a healthy reserve in an emergency fund!

Risk Mitigation through Loan Rates and Terms

There are a number of loan terms that you need to know before getting started in private lending. These rates and terms, after all, are the foundation to protect your loan. The guidelines you set here are meant to protect your capital investment and help you feel adequately compensated for the inherent risks associated with the loan. In addition to understanding what each loan term is used for, we will also share with you a philosophical approach to determining your individual private lending standards. This will take into consideration your desired outcomes from private lending as a passive investment.

The loan components you will need to define for each deal:

Total Loan Amount

This is the amount of capital being offered by the lender.

Borrower

Also known as the maker of the loan, these are the individuals or entity who will be financially liable for the repayment of the loan. The borrower seems simple enough but can be more complicated than you might think. For example, if your borrower is married and resides in a community-property state, you may need to include the spouse to acknowledge the loan or remove their interest in the property at signing.

The borrower may also be listed as a business entity or individual. *Which should you lend to?* Many experts advise only lending to business entities, as borrowers are less likely to claim it was for personal use rather than business use, invoking the claim that a usurious loan was issued. This does not mean you should not lend to an individual(s) or partners outside of an LLC. Check with your state law, but many states do not bar you from providing a commercial- or business-use loan to an individual. If you prefer to lend to a business entity, we suggest you include any members as individually named borrowers or require a personal guaranty.

The end game here is that you want to have the borrower financially responsible for the loan in addition to any business entities involved in the loan and project. This is because entities can go bankrupt and close. Most smaller businesses do not even have assets to make their entity worth much at all. Financially tying individuals to your loans ensures the borrower has more skin in the game and puts them legally on the hook should anything go wrong with the loan.

Lender Costs

This includes any loan origination, including origination points and processing costs. We know a lot of private lenders who do not charge anything to do the loan other than the pass-through of legal, title, and escrow fees. Other private lenders follow suit from hard-money lenders and charge a percentage point or two on the loan. This is purely your own choice.

Annual Interest Rate

It will be helpful for you to understand what is typically offered in your market. We suggest doing some research online about local alternative lenders and their standard ranges of rates. Just do a web search for "hard-money lenders <insert your market here>" or "real estate investor loans <insert your market or state

here>." This should provide a starting point for your competitive analysis. Once you have an idea of the prevailing rates and terms in your chosen market, you can gauge where you would like to be in relation to other lenders.

How do you know how much to charge? You will want to set your conditional rates and terms based on risk and competition. For example, if you know the majority of your competition is charging two origination points and 10 percent annualized interest, you can use that as a guidepost for pricing your loan. You can shift the loan terms to match the risk you currently perceive in the loan and structure the loan to allow for a win-win for both you and the borrower. The key here is to find the rate commensurate to the risk and competitive enough that you will not lose the loan to someone else, should you really like this deal.

Monthly Payment Terms

This is the monthly interest installment payment amount. There are several ways to collect your monthly interest installments. The most obvious is to have the monthly interest owed paid to you at the beginning of each month. However, some lenders choose to collect all interest payments at the end of the loan, when the final principal and interest payments are made. This way the borrower is never "late" and the lender doesn't have to worry about whether or not the borrower made their payment each month. Another option is to have payments prepaid at the beginning of the loan or through interest reserves. This is a way to pay the lender up front for the monthly interest so payments are not required each month.

Whether or not you choose to receive monthly payments or defer them all to the end of the loan, there is still a monthly interest amount that would be accrued each month. While there are multiple philosophies for and against taking monthly payments, we encourage you to use the monthly payment method for your first several loans, and then you can adopt other methods described here once you get used to the entire process. It is a matter of preference; however, you also need to take into account whether you need monthly installment payments to support your cost of living.

For example, we know retired couples who've sold their rental properties in favor of the more passive investment in private lending. Since they used the rental income to pay monthly bills and support their lifestyles, they wanted to continue to receive monthly payments. In other instances, however, you may elect to defer all interest payments to the end of the loan for simplicity's sake. This would be useful to a borrower who is working on a vacant flip, which will not generate any income.

We address other philosophical approaches to payments in the supplemental materials (www.biggerpockets.com/lendingbonus). For now, we want you to know two things about monthly payments: (1) if you will require monthly payments, you will need to know what that amount is and (2) you will need to define what your approach is when discussing loan terms with prospective borrowers. For the purposes of this book, we will assume monthly installment payments will be required.

After your loan funds, it is the borrower's responsibility to pay you each month as stipulated in your loan terms. To help facilitate this process, we recommend working with a third-party service provider that is an independent contractor paid to handle your monthly payments, any late notices, final payoff calculations and statement preparations, and end-of-year tax forms for both you and the borrower. The convenience factor is amazing, as they do the number-crunching and monthly check-ins for you.

While it costs some money to set up and run the account, servicers are great for handling automatic electronic payments directly from the borrower's bank account and into your specified account each month. Fees can run up to $300 for a one-time setup charge and $35 per month for an ongoing service charge. You will need to do some research on where to find a third-party servicer. There are a handful of national servicing partners, or you can find a local small bank, credit union, or escrow company that provides these services. We recommend using a servicer on your first couple of loans. If you decide it is unnecessary after that, you can always choose to service your own loans as long as it is allowed in your state. You will need to consult with a real estate attorney to understand the requirements for servicing loans in the state, as some require you to be licensed in some capacity.

We pass-through our loan servicing charges directly to the borrower, so when we talk with prospective borrowers, we let them know up front that there will be a third-party servicing company involved and to expect some nominal fees associated with it. However, the benefit to the borrower is the ability to put the loan on auto-ACH withdrawal each month, which takes a task off their plate. Another added benefit is the ability to have a 1099-INT (for interest earned) and 1098-INT (for interest paid) at the end of each year for taxes. Not all providers include this service so be sure to inquire as to what services are included in the monthly service and setup charges and what is extra.

Length of the Loan

There are a couple of schools of thought on loan durations. One is to match the loan terms with the type and scale of project being completed. If the borrower intends to flip a house in four to six months and will take an additional one to two months to put it on the market and close the sale, you may choose tight loan terms at eight months to force the borrower to stick to planned timelines. Conversely, many investors who want to keep their money working for them at all times may choose a minimum of twelve-month loan terms so they do not have to work to find another loan to fund so soon. Your goal will be to find the sweet spot that matches your borrower's timelines and meets your own investment needs.

Late Fees and Other Penalties

Depending on state law, you may choose to put punitive measures in your loan terms. The goal here would be to incentivize positive behavior by defining consequences for not following through. Whether you view these terms as a carrot approach versus a stick approach, be sure to consult with an attorney on what is considered legal and standard practice in your state.

Some punitive measures to consider include:

- **Late fees:** How long after the payment due date before the loan is considered late? You will need to define both the number of days and the penalty (typically no more than 10 percent, depending on state law).
- **Default balloon payment:** This is a penalty fee applied if the borrower defaults for any reason. You may choose to penalize the borrower a small percentage of the loan amount. Typically, this is no more than 1 to 3 percent of the total loan amount and depends on state-specific regulations. The intent of this charge is to recoup costs or collect on the loan and the loss of income from not being able to redeploy the capital on a new loan. You should consult your local real estate attorney familiar with foreclosures on what is deemed reasonable in your specific state.
- **Default interest rate:** This is the interest rate hike that occurs if the borrower should default on the loan. In some states, this can go into effect when the loan is thirty days past due, but you will need to consult with your local real estate attorney to understand how the state defines the term and the maximum rates allowed.

If any of these above terms are allowable in your state, we would encourage you to have some or all of them in your loan terms. We aren't trying to take the borrower for more money; we are ensuring there is good reason for the borrower to remit payments on time and repay you in full, as expected. Some of our independent lender friends have not included these types of terms and found that it was extraordinarily difficult to get the borrower to repay the loan. The borrower had no incentive to repay the loan when their default interest rate only went up to 6 percent from 5 percent with no other punitive costs. The borrower said they'd rather keep paying default interest because it was money they could roll over to another project.

Personal Guaranty

A personal guaranty (PG) is a legal instrument binding an individual to the loan. This is only important if the loan is made to a business entity since then you will want to have the members of the business personally held liable for the loan as well. The entity may or may not be worth anything of value. If it doesn't have income or assets and is unable to pay the loan, then a personal guaranty from the members will ensure the business members will be personally responsible for the loan instead. Like a business entity without income or assets, an individual with little to no net worth is not a strong case for a personal guaranty, so a verification of borrower assets and cash flow will be important in the Compile & Condition step.

Rehab Costs

These are the funds required to update a property. As a private lender, you will have to decide if you should disburse all rehab funds up front at the beginning of the loan or hold some back at closing. The answer will depend on your comfort level with the project and how large of a scope the work is. For smaller cosmetic rehabs, you may not want to hold any funds back. With contractors and suppliers requiring deposits, a large portion of the budget may be required quickly and up front. The intention of the holdback is to mitigate risk, not handcuff the borrower with funds you won't release because you do not understand the project's specific accounts payable. Our recommendation would be to not hold back funds on your first loan or two. This will force you to stick to straightforward cosmetic flips, which have far smaller budgets than full "studs out" renovations. Once you get the hang of it, you can take on more complex projects that may merit a rehab holdback.

That should cover most of the key loan terms you will need to contemplate in order to create the appropriate guardrails around your preferred ranges and terms, in advance. This will also help you create loan term sheets during the Contact step if you choose to proceed further with a loan.

Usury, Licensing, and Other Lender Regulations

Depending on the state you are lending from and what state the subject property is in—if those two are not the same state—you may need to evaluate if you need a license to lend or service the loan, or if you need a trustee. This becomes a very complex topic that is best handled by an attorney familiar with lending. For example, one state in the U.S. does not allow the use of any other state's usury limits and caps all loans at a very low rate for private lenders. In other states, there is no licensing required for private lenders and no usury limits! Meanwhile, some states on their own are complex and require licensing for certain types of loans with certain types of borrowers or properties, but in other categories, no licensing is required.

While this book focuses primarily on lending out your own capital, or money you directly control, another aspect to licensing that we wanted to touch upon is brokering loans. For example, if another private lender is helping you place capital, they are acting as a broker by connecting a borrower with capital that is not their own. They may require a license to do this, depending on state requirements. In addition, if you have placed all of your available money and now friends and family are wanting your help to place their capital, this may require you to be licensed to broker funds in that state. Given the amount of money at stake, spend some time with an attorney to see what is legally possible in your chosen market.

And just to further complicate licensing, some states have different licensing, such as mortgage broker versus licensed mortgage lender, or some variation thereof. You may need a broker license for one situation and a lender license for another.

Licensing and usury laws are what limit most private lenders to very specific markets. There are a lot of moving parts to remaining legal in the lending space. As a summary, some of the issues that you will need to address are state-specific licensing and compliance, federal compliance, consumer-protection compliance, and securities compliance (regulations governed by the Securities and Exchange Commission (SEC)).

Hopefully this gives you an idea as to why we are so adamant about developing some lending criteria early on. You need to know which lane to stay in and what the requirements are to remain in that lane legally. Don't feel pressured to branch out to other areas, other property types, or a different level of renovation that you are uncomfortable with just because you get a good feeling from a potential borrower. It may not be cost-effective to hire legal counsel to establish your lending parameters in a new state for one new borrower. Even the smallest of markets are likely to have plenty of opportunities to lend on residential real estate, so don't be afraid to look for the right borrower with the right property, even if it takes a few months. Make your first few loans successfully, and then, if you develop a trusted network in another market, consider moving your lending criteria to that market or including additional criteria for the new market.

Do not let this warning about the risks of private lending law scare you away! As part of every investment opportunity, there are inherent risks and rules you need to know. We bring it up first—before you get started on lending out your funds—so you can do some homework. You know the phrase "You don't know what you don't know." We're bringing up what you should know so you can go ask the right people the right questions. In fact, check out the supplemental materials at www.biggerpockets.com/lendingbonus, where we provide you with some key questions to ask a real estate attorney. Be sure you ask an attorney familiar with lending law and usury in your state.

LESSONS LEARNED

Deb is an active flipper who, like many other W-2 workers, wanted to create a second source of income for herself and her family so she could retire sooner than planned. In between projects, she was approached by an acquaintance in her real estate network with an offer to do a private loan for four months. Not knowing when she would find her next real estate project, she decided to fund this private loan for $125,000. On the surface, its attractive returns and short time frame made it seem like the perfect opportunity to keep her money earning a return until the next solid deal came along. Four months passed quickly, and Deb wondered when her funds would be returned so she could move forward with her next flip. The loan matured and ended up in default. There were verbal promises from the borrower that it would be just a small delay in repayment and that she would receive her interest owed. After a few *more* months passed by with no more communication from the borrower, Deb decided to meet with an attorney to discuss next steps. Upon reviewing her loan documents, it was discovered that the loan was not secured by any real estate or personally guaranteed by the borrower. That meant her loan did not have any real estate backing the money as collateral in case the borrower stopped paying, and the person who signed the documents did not pledge any of their personal assets to help cover the loan should the business entity default. Instead, the loan was created between her and a business entity set up by the borrower that had little to no financial holdings, making the process to recover funds much more difficult.

The biggest lesson in this transaction is to make sure the loan is secured by a property or properties with a sufficient equity buffer to protect your principal investment and to obtain a Personal Guaranty, though without verification of the borrower's assets, this could be worth no more than the paper it's written on. This secured collateral, and the sufficient equity buffer the borrower has in the property, will be your lifeline if things don't go smoothly with the repayment of your loan. This is particularly important if the borrower (either an entity or an individual) has little to no net worth to recover your funds. Foreclosures can only happen when real property is involved. If there is no real estate securing your loan, you would need to take a different course of action to recover your funds. While this is not impossible to do, it can be a much more time-consuming and complex legal process. Even if you prevail in court, getting paid after a summary judgment is not guaranteed. Think along the lines of a deadbeat parent who has been taken to court to pay back child support. Or consider the former pro NFL football player who infamously fled police after his estranged wife and her friend were stabbed to death outside her home in Santa Monica. While he successfully defended himself in the criminal case, he went on to lose a civil suit with a $33.5 million settlement to the parents of the victim. To this date, nearly two decades later, the families have not received any compensation. This is certainly an extreme case of circumstances, but the point here is to make sure you have the safest and quickest recovery plan available to you when private lending so you are capable of protecting and recovering your principal investment as easily as possible.

CALCULATE & EVALUATE IN REVIEW

C

CALCULATE & EVALUATE
In this pre-step, you will conduct a pre-assessment of your investment needs and the reasons behind why you want to get started in private lending. You will calculate your risk, evaluate your "why," and pull together some preset criteria for what you would want to see in an ideal loan.

P

PERSON
You, the lender, are the most central part of this step, as you must evaluate what matters most to you. Before lending out your hard-earned money, start with self-evaluation and then move on to the process of finding the right loan, borrower, and project.

PROPERTY
In this step, you will need to identify your baseline preferences for property or properties you would be interested and capable of lending on.

Baseline property criteria include typical property metrics such as max LTV, type of property, and condition of the property.

PAPERWORK
You will complete a Personal Private Lender Assessment to explore your private lending needs, wants, and desires.

R

RISKS AND REWARDS
Not completing this step thoroughly or at all could put you in some tough situations later down the line. If not done or not done well, you could have emotional, financial, or logistical consequences. For example, deciding to do a complex development project as your first loan could drag out the due diligence on a loan, causing delays or worse. Or maybe you take on a loan that has a loan amount close to the value of the property, which causes you to lose sleep for months.

CALL TO ACTION FOR CALCULATE & EVALUATE

1. Complete the Personal Private Lender Assessment located in the supplemental materials (www.biggerpockets.com/lendingbonus).
2. Establish your baseline loan guidelines by creating a preliminary set of loan terms that represent the acceptable ranges and terms you would like on a prospective loan opportunity.
3. Reach out to a local real estate attorney who understands private lending to learn more about your state's lending regulations, including licensure requirements, if any, and usury laws.
4. Remember your "why!" Why do you want to pursue private lending as a way of making your money work for you versus other ways of investing?

Chapter 4
CONNECT

CALCULATE & EVALUATE | **CONNECT** | CONTACT | COMPILE & CONDITION | COMPOSE & CLOSE | COLLECT & CONVEY

CONNECT QUICK PEEK

C	**CONNECT** In this step, the goal will be to make connections with people who can help build out your network of real estate professionals and potential sources of borrowers.

P	**PERSON** People. People. People. This step is all about networking. Who, where, when, and what you need from your growing real estate community.	**PROPERTY** Establish your baseline property criteria to share with prospective borrowers.	**PAPERWORK** Develop items for networking and assess legal documents, frameworks, and needs.

R	**RISKS AND REWARDS** Risks in this step could be opening your lending parameters too wide or not sharing them altogether. This will cause you to be flooded with requests for loans that do not meet your needs. Take the time to get a solid set of legal documents made and understand what they say.

In this step, you will build your network before you have a viable loan on your plate. Think of this step as lead generation for your budding business. Under typical loan sales and origination parameters, you would need to get in front of a few thousand people a month to get a handful of solid leads. From that handful of solid leads, you may find and fund just a few closed loans. While you are not an actual loan officer, the actions you take in this Connect step to prospect for new and qualified leads are very similar to these types of daily responsibilities. You are simply looking to create professional connections under a group context.

Private lending tends to be very collaborative. You're on a team with the active investor and other real estate professionals to get the deal closed. You therefore need to be on the same page in terms of quality and frequency of communication, loan terms, goals for the property, timeline for certain events, and parameters for hazard and title insurance. You also need an attorney in your corner that represents you. Nothing kills a private lending relationship faster than not being in alignment on these aspects from the very beginning.

Here are just some of the people you will want to connect with during your networking activities.

- **Active real estate investors:** This includes flippers, landlords, developers, or whoever fits into your preferred borrower profile.
- **Other private or hard-money lenders:** These are people or businesses you could partner up with in the future, if you do not have the expertise or capital to do the loan yourself.
- **Real estate attorneys:** Try to find an attorney who specializes in real estate as well as private money placement. In addition, some real estate attorneys will specialize in litigation, or foreclosure, so the attorney who draws up your documents may not be the same attorney you need to speak with if foreclosure needs to happen.
- **Title representatives:** It's always a good idea to establish a relationship with a title representative who can help answer any questions you may have regarding title commitments. Title-company employees can provide such a wealth of information!
- **General contractors:** Connecting with general contractors can be helpful when you have a complex rehab project and you want a second opinion from someone more experienced.
- **Real estate brokers:** A lot of real estate brokers are also investors. These professionals have an abundant amount of knowledge and tend to have referrals if they work directly with investors. They also know their local

market well and could help with valuation of the subject property or any planned development in the area.

- **Mortgage brokers:** Mortgage brokers are another source of referrals for people who may need private money. They can also help provide you with a better understanding of conventional mortgages as a potential exit strategy for borrowers.
- **Insurance agents:** This professional will be able to provide insight into different types of coverage for insurance and potentially examine a policy for you that a borrower has submitted.

PERSON

You don't need to know it all; in fact, there's no way you *can* know it all. You just need to know the right people. The main thing to realize is that depending on the business model you have set up for private lending and the types of loans you make, you may not want or need a resource for every role involved in a loan. Use the ones you need and disregard the ones you feel you do not. In the beginning you may go through a few of each until you build a team you can work with consistently and reliably. Finding the right virtual team to support you as a private lender will take time and effort. Eventually, you may discover you no longer need help on specific roles or aspects of the loan, and that is fine. But when starting out, we want you to know all third parties that you should have some contact or interaction with, should you need the support.

Attorney

Identifying a qualified real estate attorney familiar with lending in your market is the No. 1 priority when getting started. Remember, when you lend money, the only thing you get in return to secure that money is legally binding paperwork. Yes, you get a piece of real estate to secure the loan—but only on paper. You also get documents with the promise of repayment and additional interest. Of utmost importance is making sure the paperwork is accurate and legal and protects you as the lender. Do not skimp in this area! A few thousand dollars upfront can save you tens of thousands in litigation or principal loss.

Here are some of the qualities, skills, and areas of expertise you will need from an attorney.

- Ability to advise and guide you on state-specific usury law and lending licensure requirements

- Familiarity with and ability to draw up real estate contracts, specifically legally binding secured loans
- Proven track record of loan documents that held up in court of law when challenged
- *Bonus* if the attorney will provide you with risk reviews on certain loans when you need a second opinion
- *Bonus* if the attorney can facilitate as the closing agent on your loan as well (if allowable in your state)
- *Bonus* if the attorney can also act as the trustee over your loan(s) and support the release of your loan on the property (deed-of-trust states only and not necessary in mortgage states)

There are certain circumstances during the course of an active loan where you may require additional legal support outside the attorney you use to draft your loan documents. Some of these legal resources might be to:

- Support all the above tasks in other states you may wish to expand. Remember, lending for investment properties is regulated and governed by each individual state. If you have done a few loans in one state, do not assume the same licensing and lending regulations apply in a neighboring state. (Geraci LLP in California specializes in private lending law and can support all fifty states.)
- Facilitate the foreclosure process and/or advise on recourse options if a loan goes into default. Some loan servicing companies may help facilitate foreclosure for an additional fee for loans they are servicing.
- Advise or support bankruptcy proceedings if the borrower files for bankruptcy. Some attorneys practice both foreclosure and bankruptcy, but many do not.

We have built a trusted relationship with our local attorney, who creates each of our loan documents. He is available to provide legal advice on each deal we fund to ensure it is transacted properly. We love having this partnership with someone who has our best interests in mind. It's certainly worth the cost (which could be passed down to the borrower) to have a legal set of eyes on each deal you make and to ensure you do not have any small errors in your data entry, which could have negative consequences.

Some lenders prefer to create one set of documents as a template, which they are then able to edit with a future borrower's name and property address, along with terms for that loan. Our advice if you move forward with this approach is to make sure you have the documents reviewed periodically, as laws and regulations do change. Our preference, however, is to establish a partnership with the attorney who will create a complete set of loan documents on your behalf for each loan you fund.

It is important to mention that if you used an attorney as a closing agent to buy your home, they may not be the best resource for transactions involving private loans for investment properties. Many real estate attorneys who close conventional loans to buy a primary home are given the loan documents by the lender. As the closing agent, the attorney generally does not review the documentation before you sign it, other than to make sure everything is there that is required by law to be signed. We strongly advocate you find an attorney who specializes in this lending space in your market. They will be more familiar with the state laws and requirements for documentation that each borrower must and should have for the lending aspect of real estate transactions.

Title Officer or Representative

This will be the person(s) who pulls a title report together, usually called a "preliminary title commitment." A good title company is worth its weight in gold! You want a company that is easy to communicate with, gets items handled in a timely manner, and is willing to do some occasional out-of-the-box thinking. In a later chapter, we'll talk about potential title issues you will want to look for in a title report, but knowing you have a title company in your corner to ask questions related to the vesting of the property, any liens, encumbrances, judgments, or other exceptions, is important. Our rule of thumb is when in doubt, ask the title officer. They are considered the subject-matter expert on how to clear a title report so you can record your loan with the property as collateral. Not all title companies are created equal, so find one you enjoy doing business with and let your borrowers know as early in the process as possible that you have a preferred title company.

Escrow Closer (Closing Agent)

This is the person or entity responsible for facilitating a closing and for funding your loan. Once loan documents are ready, the closing agent prepares the loan documents for the borrower to sign, creates and finalizes the settlement statement, orders a lender title insurance policy, and funds the loan once everything is approved and ready to send to the government agency that will be recording the secured loan against the real property used as collateral. The closing agent may be the person signing the borrower (and seller, if it's a purchase transaction), or they may coordinate a mobile notary public if the parties need to sign remotely.

Many small and independent private lenders choose a do-it-yourself funding process that doesn't include the services of a closing agent. We do not recommend this approach for many reasons. One of the most important reasons is the omission or neglect to obtain a title insurance policy on do-it-yourself loans. Another issue is that documents could be notarized inaccurately and make the loan at risk of being challenged if something goes wrong. Most notaries at the bank lack sufficient knowledge or authority to properly complete your loan package. Without escrow support, the recording of the loan documents with the proper municipality office (recorder's office or clerk's office) is literally in the hands of the lender to complete and often requires doing it in person at the proper government offices. We have encountered situations where the lender forgot or delayed recording the proper documents against the real property and ended up in a junior lien (lower lien priority behind other encumbrances) because they either waited too long or didn't record it at all. Worse, we've had some lenders who allowed the borrower to be the one responsible for recording the loan documents and the borrower never followed through, making the loan unsecured by real property.

Property Insurance Agent

While the responsibility of securing insurance will fall on the borrower, you will need to make sure the property is adequately insured and that your name or company name is added to the policy as a mortgagee or loss payee. In more simplified terms, this means that you, as the lender, are listed as a beneficiary if the property is damaged in any way. If the property is destroyed completely and you are not on the insurance policy, you may or may not be entitled to any compensation from the insurance claim.

Even if the borrower uses their own insurance agent or company, having an insurance agent who will review a policy for you will help a lot in the beginning. Our insurance agent partner gladly offers to review our policies when we have questions about proper coverage. In return, if the borrower needs a referral of an agent or we need to request better coverage than their existing agent can offer, our agent is the first person we recommend. If that is not enough of an incentive, you could offer to pay them for their time to review the policy, give recommendations, or explain certain things to you. We will eventually dive into some common insurance parameters you may want included in a policy to help protect your interest in the property in case an insurable event occurs. But for now, while you are connecting with people, keep your eyes peeled for a good insurance broker.

Property Valuation Expert

When evaluating a loan opportunity, you need to establish an as-is value (current condition) and an after-repair value (ARV) on the property or properties you will use as collateral to secure the loan. There are many people who could assist you with this part of the loan process.

- **Appraiser:** An appraiser can be expensive, and their process is slow, but they are sometimes required by hard-money lenders and *always* required for conforming loans. As crazy as the real estate market has been in recent years, trying to find an appraiser who will work with you as a private lender may be a challenge, as appraisers typically have plenty of repeat work from banks and other larger lending institutions.
- **Real estate broker:** If you have a real estate agent or broker in your area with whom you want to work, you can pay them a small fee to pull together a broker price opinion (BPO) or comparative market analysis (CMA). Unlike appraisers, real estate brokers will look at comparative data but not make adjustments to each property based on more refined criteria such as square footage below grade (basements) or lack of a garage.
- **Hybrid valuation companies:** There are also third-party vendors who offer a variety of services to give you detailed breakdowns of estimated market value with supported comparison sales. The most basic offering is an online valuation tool—think Zillow's Zestimate but with more precise algorithms and user-specific customization to narrow down your comparative data with greater accuracy. However, these companies often offer additional services, including a broker price opinion, which would require a local expert to walk the property in person, either exterior only or interior as well. Some valuation companies will also offer some sort of appraisal services as well.

While you may run into many real estate brokers and a few appraisers at local real estate meetups, you will have to contact some hybrid valuation companies directly to find out more about their services and how you could become a client as a private lender.

Transaction Coordinator

This role may not be necessary when you are first starting out, but after doing a few loans, or if you increase your loan volume substantially, a coordinator might be a good investment to help you manage your loans and save you some time. This role can help facilitate activities related to loan processing all the way through the closing of the loan. This could include obtaining documentation from the borrower and coordinating with the title company, attorney, and appraiser to get the required items for closing. They can send out reminders to borrowers to submit documentation and communicate requirements with vendors, such as hazard-insurance requirements for you as a lender. This is a common resource used by real estate brokers who need assistance with listing and selling a property for a client. It is not uncommon to find contract transaction coordinators at real estate meetups and on local real estate investing social media forums who are willing to do gig work for a flat fee per loan transaction.

Loan Servicing

This company will handle the repayment process of the loan and some other back-end items like preparing tax documents for borrowers and payoff statements when the loan is to be repaid. Some will handle initiating the paperwork for the foreclosure process and also retain all original documents in a safe place so you do not lose them. There will be a small monthly fee and an onboarding process to get the documentation and account set up.

As with some legal fees, you could also consider passing these charges over to the borrower, as we do. Therefore, if you want to use a loan servicing company, try to identify the fee schedule well before placing a loan so you can set expectations with the borrower on costs and so you also know what services are included, what is offered at an additional cost, and what services are not offered at all.

SUMMING UP THE COSTS

All of these resources and vendors have charges associated with their services. The question you may be thinking is "Who'll be responsible for paying all these fees?" Many of the charges are paid out through escrow when the loan funds. Furthermore, these charges can often be paid for by the borrower. We usually inform our borrowers that there will be a processing fee that helps cover the cost of document preparation from our legal team and the loan servicing fees. If we use a transaction coordinator, we add that into our processing fees as well. Other third-party charges such as title insurance, property insurance, and escrow closing fees are expenses that borrowers are accustomed to paying at closing.

Where to Find the People

Finding the right people can be as easy or hard as you make it and will be dependent on how experienced and integrated you currently are in your local real estate community. The ability to locate the right people for your virtual team will also depend on how much time you have for networking and your overall willingness to get out there. We strongly suggest finding many of these team players before you have a deal to fund so you are not left scrambling trying to find coverage for a key player.

Real Estate Meetups and Educational Events

If you are new to real estate or new to a market, going to real estate-related networking events or talks can help you meet local people. Generally, representatives from title companies and mortgage companies and even appraisers may advertise or have a table at a local meeting as an event sponsor. You can ask other investors who they may use for certain services as well, if you are having difficulty finding good local resources on your own.

Networking with other investors in your market isn't about grilling them for who they use for various services. Other investors have experiences with other people in the local market. They may in fact share who *not* to work with more often than provide recommendations. If you hear a similar story from several investors, you should probably believe them. Remember whom you are speaking to and if you trust their information. Do they stand to gain anything from steering you toward a particular vendor? Do they have some sort of financial incentive for you to use one vendor over another? As Ronald Reagan once said, "Trust but verify."

There are also other nonverbal clues that may give you a "feeling" about a person. If you feel something is off, chances are your subconscious is picking up on cues you consciously don't recognize. Assessing borrowers in this qualitative rather than quantitative manner will yield you much better results. If you need clarification, ask for it. If you would like a connection to someone else who does a similar function, ask others for their recommendations. Watch their reactions. Do they speak poorly about other people? Someone who bad-mouths companies or vendors upon the first meeting of a total stranger isn't going to spare you the same fate. Look for the quality of character in a person rather than what they can provide in the moment. People may not always remember what you told them, but they will remember how you made them feel. Keeping open ears and an open mind at these in-person events can yield you the best results.

Online or Virtual Events

In the post-pandemic era, many people have become very comfortable with virtual networking events. These may be held on various platforms and involve listening to a speaker, being put into virtual rooms with others to exchange information, or just meeting up virtually with a small group of people to discuss a certain topic from their individual perspectives. These virtual meetups have the benefit of being done from the comfort of your home (or car!), and you can typically spend a good deal of time listening. In the beginning, listening can teach you far more than speaking. Who else shows up to these events? What do they do? How much experience do they have? Are they investing in real estate in a similar way as you? If they are in your market, how long have they been operating in your market? A limitation to virtual networking events is that many people don't think they can get the same "feel" for a person. They may want to sit down and have coffee with someone rather than spend a few minutes in the same virtual room.

Social Media and Online Platforms

Another place to connect with other investors is through social media. You can join groups or follow individuals you want to get to know or may have already met. Choose the groups you join with a purpose. Joining a national real estate investing forum might be full of posts from people all over the country, and many of the topics may not be applicable to you and your market. It can be a good way to learn the language of real estate, but it may not drill down on the specific local aspects which you are looking to learn more about. We would not recommend advertising or looking for prospective borrowers on these national real estate investing forums. Instead, focus on more localized groups where the possibility of meeting in person and visiting the property or project in question is greater.

If you join a smaller local group, this can be a great way to connect with other private lenders in your market or receive recommendations to fill any remaining gaps in your virtual team. It can also be a tool to begin screening potential borrowers. Seeing what they post on social media may give you a peek into how they think and what they spend their time doing. If you are a member of a group on social media, you can read through posts and responses to those posts to get a feel for the sentiment an individual conveys to the group. Are they confrontational in the group? Do they call people names? Do they add value or offer a different way of looking at the topic? Do they seem knowledgeable on the subject matter? You could always reach out to someone individually on social media and arrange a time to chat if allowed by the group.

Joining groups for both your market and your style of investing gives you a general pulse on the topics or events relevant to those subjects. Even if you are not actively involved in real estate investing, you will still underwrite your deals as a lender, which will utilize some of the same metrics and factors. For example, if new legislation within your chosen market changes, such as tenants' rights adversely affecting landlords, being in a local landlord group—even if you don't own rental property—may be advantageous. Your borrowers may want to purchase a property to turn into a rental, and you as the lender need to be able to analyze how viable their rental property exit strategy really is given this new legislation. This may be especially pertinent if you are lending to someone who wants to make the subject property a short-term rental. Some markets change legislation frequently, and in some specific jurisdictions, these types of rentals are forbidden altogether. Knowing this key piece of information ahead of time can save you and your borrower some heartache before closing.

Joining groups specifically for lenders can help, as you can get referrals to lender-specific vendors as well as potential leads on borrowers in your market. For example, other private lenders may not have the capital available for a borrower at the right time; otherwise they would happily lend to that individual. If you are another lender in the network of that community, they may have a referral for you and give you a warm introduction to a borrower they have loaned to in the past.

Finally, private lending social media groups can provide a place to ask questions specific to lending or to solicit recommendations for vendors. Some groups play a role in advocacy for private lending, so any pending legislation changes may be discussed in these types of groups as well. These local social media groups can also be a good place to ask others what in-person real estate events or meetups exist and are worth attending.

BiggerPockets Forums

BiggerPockets.com is a great place to connect with local and national investors of all types. The forums are broken down by various categories, including location (city/state versus national), topic, and industry updates. There is a specific forum for private lending under the Loans, Mortgages, and Credit Lines topic. And you can find other useful information and topics, including creative financing, self-directed IRAs, and more. BiggerPockets has a presence on Facebook and Instagram as well.

Private Lending Industry Events

There are a lot of private lending events throughout the year that could help you become more versed in private lending trends and practices. This is also a great way to find additional vendors or individuals to add to your virtual team. Some of these events include:

- **American Association of Private Lenders (AAPL) annual conference:** This event is typically held in the fall in Las Vegas and is well-attended by new, aspiring, and established lenders of all sizes and types. We love this event because it's put on by an established organization dedicated to education, advocacy, and ethics.
- **Geraci LLP media events:** This national law firm, which specializes in private lending, holds two events annually—one in the spring in Southern California and another larger event at the end of the summer in Las Vegas.
- **National Lending Experts (NLE) conferences:** With several events a year, NLE is committed to connecting real estate investors, brokers, lenders, and service providers while delivering up-to-date information on market conditions and trends in private lending.
- **Pitbull conference:** This is one of the oldest private money conferences. Founder Leonard Rosen holds events several times a year with a mission to facilitate commerce between capital providers, lenders, investors, brokers, and service providers.

Alternative Solutions to Consider

We did say this would be mostly passive as an investment strategy, but in the beginning, there is work to do and people to connect with. If you're someone who, for whatever reason, prefers not to work or socialize with other people, but you still want to have some money in the private lending space, you might consider alternatives to directly lending your own money. Although the saying "your network is your net worth" is a little overused, it is very true in the private lending business. If you are not comfortable with networking or if you have little time to do so, it may be a challenge to find and fund quality loans by yourself. Consider these options if you feel it may be difficult to create the virtual team needed to execute a private loan on your own.

Using a Direct Private Money Lender to Place Your Funds

One option is to have your capital brokered through a trusted private money direct lender instead of placing it yourself. If you choose to go this route, we recommend you read this book so you have baseline information and knowledge about the lending process and can therefore evaluate the best deal to fund. Working with a trustworthy and knowledgeable broker who can help underwrite a file, gather required material, and call on an already established network of support professionals might be an advantage if you don't feel comfortable doing the first few loans alone.

Partnering with an Experienced Private Lender

You could also partner up with another person with more lending experience. You could both fund a loan that satisfies the risk tolerances and terms you are looking for. There are a few different ways to structure this option. Best practice would be to have an attorney who is familiar with private lending to help steer you in the right direction. Partnering with another lender who knows the "rules of the road" may also teach you new aspects of that local market or introduce you to connections within their network. It would be important for you to ensure your needs and wants match that of the partner you select to work with since you will both need to agree on rates, terms, types of loan(s) to fund, etc. Later on in the book, we will discuss different ways to structure this type of partnership.

Investing in a Private Debt Fund

You could invest in a private debt fund, also known as a pooled mortgage fund. This is the most passive of all three options. A debt fund will allow you to place capital in a pool with other investors. That capital is then deployed according to the legal documentation you sign at the time of placing the capital. Depending on how the debt fund is structured, you may not know which loans the fund manager will originate, but your capital will be working the entire the duration of the agreed hold time for the fund. That means you don't have to search out additional borrowers with timelines that work out with your capital being returned to you. The lending guidelines for the fund are also spelled out in a legal document you can review prior to investing. This is called a "private-placement memorandum." This method may be favorable if you want to remain as passive as possible and not worry about the turnover between borrowers, collecting payments, or even underwriting a specific loan.

As you can see, private lending is very flexible, and it is a matter of what you want to spend your time doing, how involved you want to be in the decision-making process, and if you want to scale a private lending business now or in the future.

PROPERTY

Hopefully by now you can see why establishing your lending criteria in the Calculate & Evaluate pre-step is so crucial. You need a solid idea of what you will lend on and for how long, as well as what terms you will require in order to lend before connecting with people. Narrowing focus on the type(s) of property you are willing to lend on also allows the people you have been networking with to know exactly what you are looking for.

When speaking to others about your lending criteria, you may be tempted to keep things very vague and loose so you can be exposed to as many deals to fund as possible. What you will find is that you will be offered anything and everything under the sun unless you are specific. People will pitch you construction deals, strip malls, large multifamily, raw land, and maybe even a farm. The sky is the limit. (There will also be people who want to sell you a bunch of hot air too!)

Be as specific as you can be, but within the general parameters allowable in your market. For example, if you live in an area where the average home price is $500,000 and you only want a first lien position loan for $100,000, your desired loan may be tough to find. We aren't saying don't look for these types of opportunities, but be comfortable with having your capital sit on the sidelines until that perfect borrower and property come across your path.

Property Criteria Checklist for the Connect Step

Remember some of the property considerations we had you review during the Calculate & Evaluate stage? Before attending any networking events, you will want to have this baseline criteria prepared and perhaps documented so that you can easily share with people you meet. Below are some of those datapoints you will need to have predetermined; we've also created a sample worksheet for you to complete in the supplemental materials at www.biggerpockets.com/lendingbonus.

Type of residential properties you will lend on	My preferences are: ☐ Detached single-family homes ☐ Condominiums, townhouses ☐ Manufactured homes, mobile homes ☐ Small multifamily (two to four family units) ☐ Other: _____
Loan size range	From $ _____ to $ _____
Maximum loan-to-value	Maximum LTV is: _____ %

Property condition	☐ Cosmetic fixers ☐ Major rehabs ☐ Rehab in progress (down to the studs) ☐ Teardown (uninhabitable) ☐ Rent-ready (stabilized) only ☐ Other: _____
Location	Describe preferred property locations by geography: state, county, city, neighborhood(s), and any other criteria you see as important
Other considerations	Age of property Waterfront or flood-zone properties Rural versus metropolitan areas Population size and demographic Purchase price range

This is just the baseline property parameters you should think through before attending events and putting yourself out there as a private lender. If you have more details about what you will lend on and what you will not, great! If you do not, we will cover more about property specifics later in Chapter Ten on underwriting the property. For now, this is just the short list of property-specific lending guidelines you should establish up front.

While you do not want to bend your lending criteria to fit the market, ask yourself why you chose your specific criteria in the first place. You may know *why* you are comfortable only lending on a certain age of home, but when you connect with an investor who invests in older homes, don't hesitate to gain insight into their business model. Some investors like older homes because they hold character, which modern homes often don't have. Maybe they specialize in restoring the original beauty of an old Craftsman-style home and have a specific construction crew familiar with the details and building materials of these older homes. Or perhaps it's just that older homes are typically what is available for fix-and-flip projects. If your fear of lending on an older home was the increased costs in renovations or just the unknown that comes from opening the walls of an aged structure, listening to an investor talk about how they specifically invest in older homes and how they handle the project may put your mind at ease.

If you are looking for a general framework on typical lending guidelines, talk to other private lenders and examine the standards of hard-money lenders in your area. These insights will give you an idea of what others have experienced as well as the current prevailing rates and property criteria other lenders are willing to lend on. For example, if you are not willing to lend on a property in a flood zone, why? Are you worried about flood insurance rates getting so expensive that the demand for this type of property will fall and thus affect its value or cash flow negatively? Asking other lenders about their opinions on flood zones will help you rationalize your property preferences.

PAPERWORK

In the Connect step, very little paperwork is required because most of the focus will be on meet and greets and small talk at events. You do not want to come across as overly structured and stiff, so it's important you keep things more casual and engage with others on a personal level before diving right into business. Regardless of how you decide to network and connect with others in the real estate and private lending world, being organized in this step is critical to staying on top of things, especially when you start to do more loans.

Nowadays, everything from the loan application to the bookkeeping has been automated and digitalized. Some of the recommendations we have below are more systems than paper-based methods. The key here is to have some method picked out that works for you. If you are old-school, then use pen and paper. If you are savvy and have a systems background like us, you will likely embrace new technologies to streamline and manage your efforts during the Connect step.

Business Cards or Other Personal Contact Information

If you plan to attend several in-person events, having something simple like a business card to give people may be of value. There are even digital business card services for those who may be tech-friendly. Regardless of the media you choose, you should have some way to exchange contact information with others when attending events in person.

Customer Relationship Management (CRM)

One necessary aspect you may not have thought about quite yet is a way to track communication with people. This may be something as low-tech as a notebook to record names, contact information, and some notes about your conversation, all the way up to paid customer relationship management (CRM) services you can connect directly to your email and phone contacts. Being able to remember whom you spoke to and the topic of that discussion can be valuable to track when you're trying to get something closed on a tight timeline or when you're funding multiple loans at the same time. Just make sure you have some way of recording notes or referral sources, as it will make your life much easier down the line should you need to access that information later.

Videoconferencing Tools

Having some familiarity with videoconferencing software can also be helpful. You can jump on a video call with someone and talk face-to-face to learn more about them and what they offer. During the pandemic, a lot of real estate investor networking happened over videoconference tools such as Zoom and Google Meet. If you do not know of any digital meetups occurring, try asking on social media forums you belong to. You might be surprised by how many events take place on a regular basis.

Your Elevator Pitch

Being able to effectively share with others who you are, what you do, and what you are looking for in a lending opportunity will be important. You will need to think about how you will introduce yourself succinctly in the form of an elevator pitch. This does not have to be super formal; you simply want to explain who you are and what you do in thirty seconds or less. This sounds easy, but if you do not have the "gift of gab" like some, you will want to spend some time putting pen to paper. This exercise alone will help you articulate your goals and business plan to others in a meaningful and understandable way.

Application and Loan Documents Template

Start evaluating any standard paperwork you may want a borrower to fill out, such as a loan application, and get some legal loan documents drawn up with your attorney, if you have one identified already. Since time is critical for investors, you do not want to wait until after you have found a borrower and a deal to start work on your loan document templates. This could be an iterative and time-consuming process, depending on the availability of your attorney. Plan to start this process while you are out there connecting and networking with others.

In addition to having documents ready to go as soon as you find a deal, the insight from the attorney drawing up these documents can help guide future conversations with borrowers. For example, they can articulate why you need to remain under a usury limit for a certain type of loan or why you should lend to a business entity instead of an individual. This can help you weed out potential borrowers who insist upon vesting properties in their own names. The attorney-prepared documents can also spur questions you may not have considered before about loan terms, who and how the borrower will sign the documentation, and what the process may be to get the title to the property, should the loan default. Making the connection early with the attorney who will prepare the loan documents can shape your lending criteria for borrowers and properties in ways that reading a book alone cannot.

We will talk more in-depth about the loan application in Chapter Five and the loan documents specifically in Chapter Seven, but for now it's important to start the process of having the loan document templates drafted or finding the attorney who will do the entire document preparation for you on each file.

RISKS AND REWARDS

In our experience, private-money and hard-money lenders always tend to be some of the most popular people in the room at real estate meetups. There always seems to be an endless pool of investors seeking capital partners. The reward for connecting with others at events like these—both in person and online—is you automatically have access to warm leads who could become your next borrower. You will also be rewarded with referrals and recommendations to vendors and potential partners, as well as constructive feedback or outright warnings on who to avoid working with on future deals. The real estate investing community, even in the larger metropolitan markets, is incredibly small. Everyone seems to know each other, so becoming part of this tight-knit community can yield some interesting facts and fictions about who to know and who to keep at a distance.

Your Reputation

The risks of not getting out and connecting with people and businesses in the real estate investing community are pretty straightforward and we have addressed quite a few of those in this chapter. Not being clear on what you can offer, who you need support from, and which relationships you can lean on down the road can lead you to operating your lending business in a vacuum and cause you stress, both emotional and financial. As it's commonly said in the construction field, "Measure twice, cut once." In the private lending world, your measurements are the Calculate & Evaluate pre-step and the Connect step. Once you do both of these planning activities, you will be ready to jump right in to the actual loan origination process.

Your reputation is everything in real estate, especially in private lending. If you talk to a borrower and tell them you will fund the loan under a certain set of circumstances, then you need to perform. They are banking on you and your money showing up on closing day to fund the purchase of the property. If you leave too many borrowers at the table without the funds to close, you'll have an increasingly difficult time placing money with experienced investors. Once you get a reputation of unreliability, it can be hard to shake.

Make sure you say what you are going to do and then follow through. This includes being able to say no, even to someone you personally like. Stringing along a borrower and asking for more and more documentation wastes everyone's time. Be direct and to the point. If you are uncomfortable with an aspect of the loan, talk about it with the borrower. If they respond defensively or argumentatively, they aren't your ideal borrower. Remember you are on a team with them, and if they don't play nice at the beginning, chances are the relationship won't get better.

The last risk we want to mention here pertains to attending live private lending events. While there are several you could attend, diving into these without having some foundation may feel overwhelming. If you can network with other private lenders, you can ask about their experience at any of the events they have attended. The annual American Association of Private Lenders event hosts live educational classes before the conference. Other conferences may focus largely on interactions with vendors that may not be appropriate for an individual lending out their own capital, as these vendors tend to work exclusively with larger lenders who access capital through a fund, warehouse line of credit, or by selling their loans shortly after closing. These events can be a great way to meet multiple lenders in a short span of time but attending them too early in your lending journey may make a live event a bit overwhelming. Participating in these events can be a risk and a reward! Just be prepared and have an open mind about the experience. Private lending can sometimes feel very lonely because many who invest in real estate who are attending your local REIA meetings are doing fix-and-flips or rentals, so having these congregations of private lenders at live events is the perfect opportunity to learn more about the business of lending and meet others who chose to invest in the same way.

LESSONS LEARNED

A local private money broker in the area, Mason, proactively attends real estate events in his market and is known well in the area. He talks about his loan products, rates, what type of property he can lend on, and how quickly he can close. Additional services Mason offers for newer investors is helping them locate a property as well as placing their capital with potential borrowers. He's been in business for a number of years, and from the outside he seems like a perfect resource for someone to learn the ropes of lending in this market.

A new investor in the local area, Jackson, decided to let Mason place some of his capital for him. He wanted some passive monthly income to help bolster the household income while looking for a job. Since Mason was at many of the local real estate events and several people knew him, Jackson felt safe placing capital with him. He was public about his business and such an integral part of the real estate process (lending!), so Jackson felt this was the perfect opportunity to learn more about the market, get his capital working, and enjoy some passive income.

Jackson didn't understand much about lending but felt reassured by Mason's experience. After signing some legal documents with Mason's company, Jackson wired $200,000 to the account listed in the paperwork. He assumed it was going directly to purchase a property in the local market because Mason had so many connections in the area. Mason signed a promissory note and an explanation of how much his monthly payments and interest rate would be for the loan, and Jackson was excited he'd be making an extra $2,000 a month.

The loan was for twelve months, and for several months, the $2,000 was deposited in his bank account on time as agreed. On the fourth month, the loan payment came in late, but it was still the agreed $2,000. Mason let it slide since the other payments had come in on time. By the fifth month, the payment wasn't made until the twenty-seventh of the month—again the same $2,000. Jackson was expecting some additional late fees since this payment was so late. To Jackson's surprise, there were not any late charges written into the promissory note.

Jackson reached out to Mason for an explanation about the increasingly late payments. The first was just a few days from this latest payment, and he wanted to make sure that was coming on time as agreed. His phone call went unanswered, and Jackson sent multiple emails. A few days after the last email, Mason wrote back that a payment would be sent by the end of the day. That made Jackson happy, but it did not address why the payments were getting later and later and that made him uneasy. By the end of the week, a payment had still not been received in Jackson's account.

Jackson felt it was time to sit down and figure out what was going on. He connected with another private lender at a virtual networking event. They had multiple Zoom conversations over the past month, and he felt that this lender was pretty knowledgeable. Jackson asked if they would look over the loan documents for him to see if there was anything Jackson could do about the payments.

Jackson had thought his loan had funded the purchase of an investment property for a specific borrower. In reality, he had made a loan to Mason's business, and it was not secured by property at all! Since the lending community tends to be pretty small, Jackson's private lender friend reached out to some other people in their network and found someone who had lent money to Mason in the past. It turns out that Mason had a reputation in the local area for not being able to close loans with active investors. Most active investors with any experience in the area knew not to even fill out an application with Mason's company because he could never close the deal on time. Many shared experiences that were eerily similar, so the poor performance was pervasive throughout his business. Since the money Jackson loaned went to the business itself instead of property, there was no way to push for foreclosure by defaulting on the note. There wasn't an asset to back up the loan!

After several months of no payments, Jackson finally involved an attorney to get his $200,000 back from Mason's business. Since the loan was written for a twelve-month term, the loan still had a few months left before the balloon payment was due. The loan was in default due to nonpayment, but the attorney didn't give Jackson good odds of being able to get the full amount back.

Meanwhile, Jackson learned that the loans Mason had been closing were for brand-new real estate investors and not even in the same state as Jackson and Mason. He had no idea where his $200,000 had gone, but the idea that some of it may have been placed into risky loans didn't ease his fear. Jackson eventually found other investors in the area who had done the same loan with Mason, and they shared equal frustration with late payments or no payments at all. Even a few had loans that were past the loan term and still had not been paid.

During the litigation process, it was discovered that many of the loans made to these out-of-state investors had defaulted. The state process for foreclosure was several months long in that area, so without adequate income coming in, Mason was unable to pay his investors their payments. Also, since Mason didn't have the title to the properties, he had no right to sell them to get the initial capital back to the individual investors like Jackson.

Like we mentioned earlier, your reputation as a lender is just as important as an active investor's reputation in a given market. If the experienced investors in the area say to avoid a certain vendor, listen. There is a reason! Do not rely on the comfort of seeing someone repeatedly at a local event as credibility for their business. Second, know exactly what you are signing. If Jackson had an attorney familiar with private lending review the documents before he funded the loan, he would have known what he was getting into from the beginning.

CONNECT IN REVIEW

C	**CONNECT** In this step, the goal will be to make connections with people who can help build out your network of real estate professionals and to find the right prospective borrower(s) to lend to on your first deal.

	PERSON	**PROPERTY**	**PAPERWORK**
P	People. People. People. This step is all about networking. Attending real estate association meetups, networking, and connecting through social media real estate investing and private money lending forums can help connect you to the right people who could be potential borrowers or be referral sources for qualified borrowers.	You will need to have your baseline property criteria established to share with prospective borrowers and referral sources so they know what you are looking for. It will be important to quickly weed out those who do not fit your criteria.	You will need business cards for your networking efforts, and you will need to start looking for legal resources who can advise and create the legal paperwork required to fund a loan.

R	**RISKS AND REWARDS** Networking at local real estate events can be a terrific way to find referrals to those who need private lenders. It can also be a great way to meet other investors who may be able to provide guidance in the future when you need a second opinion from someone more seasoned in active real estate investing. Risks in this step could be opening your lending parameters too wide or not sharing them altogether. This will cause you to be flooded with requests for loans that do not meet your needs. You may become overwhelmed and confused by all the different opportunities with no real way to compare them side by side.

CALL TO ACTION FOR CONNECT

After reading this chapter, you will need to:

1. Identify what team members you currently have in your network and what roles you will still need to look for at events or online.
2. Determine what real estate investing meetups, events, webinars, and other in-person networking opportunities are in your market that you could attend.
3. Start joining forums on BiggerPockets to discuss private lending or the investment strategy you may want to focus on (such as flipping or BRRRR investing) to learn the language and connect with active investors.

4. Outline your preferred borrower profile and your preferred property criteria.
5. Order business cards or another option that suits you and will allow you to easily share your contact information with participants at these events.
6. Identify a solution for organizing your contacts and tracking your conversations.
7. Develop a thirty-second elevator pitch about who you are as a private lender and what you are looking to fund.
8. Find and retain an attorney who can prepare your loan document template specific to your preferred market(s).

Chapter 5
CONTACT

CALCULATE & EVALUATE > CONNECT > **CONTACT** > COMPILE & CONDITION > COMPOSE & CLOSE > COLLECT & CONVEY

CONTACT QUICK PEEK

C

CONTACT
In this step, the goal will be to make introductory contact with your identified prospective borrower to determine if you would want to proceed with this borrower and/or property.

P

PERSON
The main person in this step will be the potential borrower. You will be learning more about them as an investor, the project and their experience.

PROPERTY
You will be doing baseline information-gathering for the subject property, such as address, current condition, amount of work needed on the property, and an estimated value once renovated.

PAPERWORK
There are some documents you will want to collect from the borrower if the initial information fits your lending criteria.

R

RISKS AND REWARDS
There aren't usually many risks associated with the Contact step. This is your chance to "pre-qualify" a borrower and their project to see if it'll be a good fit for you. The more thorough you are in this step, the less time you will waste collecting and reviewing additional documents later.

After you begin connecting and networking within the real estate investing community, chances are you will be engaged in some informative conversations with other investors and vendors who can help you on your private lending journey. What you have been focused on up to this point is getting your name out there, collecting information, and creating meaningful connections with others. While the Connect step is about one-to-many activities (you and many investors and referral sources), the Contact step is all about one-to-one communication with individual investors or with referrals who could result in a lending opportunity.

Once you find a prospect that meets some of the general criteria you established for yourself in the Calculate & Evaluate pre-step, the next step is learning more about your prospective borrower and their respective property and project. You will need to gather some basic information and getting a better *feel* for your prospect as a person and investor. As you go through this process you will discover that some qualitative characteristics cannot really be summed up in a book. If you get a gut feeling about someone, trust it. If at any point something doesn't feel right, ask those in your network about the situation or contact your real estate attorney. Remember, you don't have to go it alone!

Everyone wants to invest with people they know, like, and trust, so you may already have some prospects from your existing network. However, just because you know someone on a personal level does not mean you shouldn't dive a little deeper. Think about a good friend you trust implicitly. They may be someone you have known for years, but do you know them professionally? How much do you know about their experience in real estate investing? Do you know their credit score? Probably not. We will point out some instances where these additional datapoints can clue you in to their potential for repayment or their capacity to respond (or not respond) when things get tough. No matter the experience level a borrower may claim to have, no renovation project ever goes exactly as planned, nor do they have full control of every variable of construction, the real estate market, or the other players involved in this project. Even if there is minimal renovation required, just getting a quality paying tenant into the unit can be its own challenge.

During the Contact step, you will establish on a very high level if this borrower and property are something you would lend on—before diving into the harder task of evaluating a ton of borrower-supplied documentation. Here we are trying to create a 30,000-foot overview. If you hear satisfactory answers to your questions, you will proceed to the next step, which will further substantiate what facts and feelings you've established in this step.

This step will involve three parts.

1. Contacting the borrower and discussing their high-level loan needs, borrower profile, and property details.
2. Completing basic administrative tasks to prepare for a loan opportunity, including calculating project financials (profit margin, after-repair values, and estimated rehab costs to assess overall project risk).
3. Preparing a preliminary term sheet for the borrower, should you wish to proceed to the next step with the loan.

The Pre-Qualification Conversation

In the Calculate & Evaluate step, we looked at what your lending criteria may be. In this step, you are evaluating potential lending opportunities and how well they match up to the personal deal preferences you established. Hopefully you can see now why it is necessary to think about your loan terms and criteria before talking to a borrower. Thinking through the different variables of private lending and knowing which are dealbreakers for you and which you might concede on will be crucial to successfully selecting your first loan to fund. For example, one requirement for many private lenders is that the property will not be occupied by the borrower at any point, since this would make the loan personal in use and, therefore, subject to state and federal consumer-protection laws. This would be a great example of a lending requirement you are unwilling to waiver on unless you are willing to keep your rates and terms lower than state usury requirements and complete the additional disclosures necessary for consumer protection. For the sake of this book, we are focused on business or commercial loans to real estate investors.

Before you begin reviewing a stranger's financials and plans for a property, there are some key questions to ask your prospective borrower that will help you identify any potential red flags or nonstarters. Much like conducting an interview with a job candidate, you will want to keep your questions more open-ended so you do not receive a bunch of yes or no responses. The key here is to ask questions that elicit a more detailed response. Your job will be to actively listen and pay attention to verbal and nonverbal cues.

Remember, this is going to be an iterative process similar to peeling off layers of an onion. If you request a whole bunch of paperwork right out of the gate, you may find yourself overwhelmed with information overload. Similarly, you could take a lot of time to request and review prospective borrower documentation and think they look excellent on paper, only to find out you cannot stand to be in the same room as them when you meet them in person. Take your time to request and review chunks of data one layer at a time. It starts with how closely this lending opportunity meets what you are looking for in the first place!

Here are the first three questions every lender needs to ask before moving on to the next layer of information:

1. How much money do you need to borrow and how much of your own capital will you be using?
First you want to find out how much the potential borrower is looking for versus how much of their own money they will infuse into the project. A safer loan is one with a low loan-to-value so there is a strong equity buffer protecting the property. A loan can also be considered safer when the borrower uses their own money on the project. In our opinion, it's too easy for the borrower to walk away from a project when things go wrong if they do not have any "skin in the game." Ultimately, the question you are trying to answer here is related to the financial risks and if the property loan-to-value falls within your personal lending guidelines.

2. Where do you live currently and will you move into the property at any point?
The borrower should not have plans to move into the property at any point, and we recommend having them put this in writing with a handwritten letter called a Borrower Strategy Form. We will explain more in the Paperwork section of this chapter, but we want to establish this up front because the parameters that afford you the most flexible lending terms are only for business-purpose loans. In layperson's terms, this means you are only lending on investment property, and the funds must be used for business purposes, such as buying and renovating an investment property. There are many more stringent requirements for lending on owner-occupied homes, both in terms of disclosures that must be made to the borrower and the interest rate and fees that can be charged to that borrower.

From a logistical standpoint, it is also helpful to know where the project is in proximity to the borrower's primary residence. If the borrower lives in Seattle and is telling you about their project in Spokane (300 miles on the other side of the state of Washington), you may want to ask some follow-up questions about how often they plan to visit the jobsite, who will be acting as the general contractor, and what experience the investor has in the Spokane market, if any.

3. What is your project plan and exit strategy? How long will the project take, how do you plan to repay the loan, and what other important financial information about your project should I know?

The third key question is what the borrower intends to do with the property once they own it. The plans for the property during their term of ownership while your loan is outstanding is called their "exit strategy." For instance, the borrower wants to renovate the property and then sell it to a buyer who will use it as their primary home. Another common exit strategy is the borrower refinances out of your private loan within a specified time frame and into a long-term conventional loan to keep the property as a rental. It is called an exit strategy because this is where you (the lender) and the borrower (the investor) exit the deal. You want a borrower to have a clear idea of what they will do with the property, backed up by experience and relevant data such as recent comparable sales for fix-and-flips or a pre-approval letter from a bank showing they are eligible to receive a conventional loan to keep the property as a rental.

Answers to these three simple questions can help you determine if the deal is something you would like to move forward with or not. The process to compile and review documentation from the borrower can be tedious, so do not waste unnecessary time on this task should the prospective borrower provide unfavorable responses to the three questions above. We recommend first asking these questions verbally during a phone conversation or in person, if possible, rather than over email or another written format. This gives you a chance to gauge the borrower's body language and ask follow-up questions easily.

PERSON

The most important person in this step is your potential borrower. You will want to have a private follow-up meeting after an initial group meeting to discuss the specifics of the opportunity and get to know each other a little better. This could be meeting in person, having a phone call, grabbing coffee, meeting at the property itself—whatever each party is comfortable with at that time. Before your initial meeting, you may not be officially requesting any sort of documentation. Your time may be best spent getting a feel for this person on a qualitative level. If you are already comfortable with the person because they are in your established network or you've already had a successful meeting with them previously, you may want to request certain documents before meeting up, such as an application and specific property details.

Think about the kind of person you would want in your corner in a dire situation. If something goes wrong, are they going to step up or bury their head in the sand? Do they paint the perfect picture of past deals, claiming they went exactly as planned? Do they blame business partners, contractors, appraisers, and anyone else but themselves for a deal not working out? How did they solve past problems? What sort of skills do they possess to take on the type of project they are seeking funding for? Have they invested in this market specifically before? Where else do they invest? What are their personal goals for real estate investing?

This initial meeting will be the first of many conversations with the borrower if you decide to move forward. If you do a loan with someone, you are involved with them financially for at least the length of the loan, and possibly longer. You want some assurances that this person is going to maintain communication with you when things are good *and* bad. You want to figure out if they will be forthcoming with challenges and do everything in their power to repay the full loan amount and the interest owed.

When you are getting to know anyone—whether personal or professional—you are gauging signs of honesty, integrity, and character. Some key traits you want to look for in a prospective borrower, both in verbal responses and body language, are good communication skills, project organization and articulation, personal accountability and focus on solutions and financial acumen. If you start hearing things that trouble you, ask more questions to get clarification on the issue. If the borrower starts getting defensive, avoids an answer, or does not have a reasonable explanation for not knowing the answer yet, that could be a sign there is a backstory they are not sharing with you.

Online Presence/Web Searches

Before meeting with prospective borrowers, we try to do a little online research about the person first. They may have posts on social media about their most recent projects or they may spend an exorbitant amount of time bashing political views. Perhaps when you do a web search, you find that they are named on a few court cases as the petitioner, which could lead you to believe they might be litigious in nature. Regardless of what you find out, it's always a good idea to see what sort of online presence your prospective borrower has before you meet up in person. It may help you to formulate additional questions you want to ask based on things you found online.

Other Common Red Flags

- **The no-show:** Even if the borrower is late, this can be an indication of poor time management on a project or how they value others' time.
- **The rambler:** While this just may be the way some people talk, it can sometimes be a sign that this person does not listen well or may be a time

suck. Some lenders do not like the "rambler" because the borrower may need to be babysat.

- **The smooth talker:** Beware of someone who acts like the consummate salesperson but does not offer up details. These types of investors can make every deal sound amazing and typically blame-shift or tell you they have never lost money or had a project go sideways.
- **The know-it-all:** There is a difference between being knowledgeable and arrogant. Some investors will try to make you feel small to showcase their strengths and talents. We prefer confidence and humility above egocentrism and condescension.

Now that we have covered some of the qualitative things to look out for during your first conversation with a prospective borrower, let's dive into the tangible things you will need to discuss as well.

Borrower Experience

During the meeting, talk about the experience the borrower may have with this type of property and renovations. Ideally, you want a borrower who has done at least a few projects similar in scope to the one they are seeking funding for, especially if you are new to real estate investing yourself. A borrower who has built a business around real estate investing has an additional incentive to perform on the loan because it is their way of making a living. In addition, if they operate in your market on a larger scale, they have an established reputation in the real estate community and won't want to jeopardize this with a defaulting loan. We've already discussed how having a good reputation in your chosen market can affect you as a lender, but it is equally important for active investors who will be your borrowers.

The experience you are looking for should be comparable to what they will be doing with the subject property. For example, the borrower may have purchased three investment properties that were turnkey. That means they bought the property already renovated and likely with a paying tenant in place. While they technically are a real estate investor because they own investment property, their prior experience doesn't involve management of a renovation with multiple moving parts, such as contractors and subcontractors accessing the home and ordering supplies for the projects. If the subject property needs extensive renovation but they have only owned turnkey rentals, that isn't similar experience in our eyes.

Project Team Members

There are many roles involved in the success or failure of a real estate investment project. Be sure to discuss with your prospective borrower who will be participating on this project and who else will be vested on the title. Depending on the type of project, you will need to know who will be acting in the following capacities.

- Other vested owners (the people on the title to the property)
- Capital or credit partners and personal guarantors
- General contractor (GC) and potential subcontractors
- Real estate broker (who will list the property for sale, if it is a fix-and-flip)
- Property management company (if the property will become a rental)
- Lender who will do the bank financing (if the property will become a rental)

While you may choose not to directly contact each of the partners or vendors involved in the project, asking the borrower to share this information with you at this point in the process can help you discern how connected they are to the project details and how far along in the planning process they are. If the borrower has not secured a general contractor, for example, you may choose to hold off funding the loan until you know more about who the general contractor will be, whether they are sufficiently licensed, bonded, and insured, and what their overall scope of work and estimated budget will be.

Most lenders only want to make a single loan to encompass some or all of the costs of acquisition and rehab. Not knowing who will be acting as the general contractor, when they can start on the project, and what the overall estimated costs may be could mean the lender will have to fund a second loan in the middle of the project to take care of budget overruns or scheduling delays, just to get the project across the finish line.

Borrower Lifestyle and Motivations

Another key factor to weigh is related to the prospective borrower's lifestyle and motivations for being in real estate. Is she a mother of four with a full-time executive-level job that is very demanding and requires overtime? Does he have three other flip projects going on right now and is therefore stretched for time and commitment? Are they telling you about the extended vacations they will be taking in the next six months? Getting to know the prospective borrower's lifestyle can help you better understand if they have the necessary time, motivations, and drive to complete a project successfully.

Business References

These professional references are people who have done business with your potential borrower in some capacity in real estate. Remember: Real estate is a relatively small community, and chances are, if your borrower has any sort of experience in a given market, they will know someone who can attest to their experience. References can be a broker who sold the borrower a home or listed the completed flip. It may be another investor they have partnered with in the past or a real estate professional, such as a mentor, whom they have an established relationship with. You can even ask if they have ever worked with other private lenders and request to speak to them. Asking who they have worked with in the past and hearing how they speak about these people can help provide some insight as to how well they play with others.

PROPERTY

While you are meeting with the borrower, or at least having initial conversations with them, you are likely going to want to know some details about the property (and project) itself. The lending criteria you set up earlier can help guide you through the pertinent information you will need to assess now. You want to assess the financial risk the property may present to both the borrower and to you as the lender. The borrower may have the intention of doing one thing with the property, but sometimes things do not go as planned, so a safer option would be to loan on a property with multiple realistic and reasonable exit strategies. If the borrower cannot qualify for bank financing by the end of the loan term, will the property still sell for a high-enough amount to pay off the loan and cover closing costs for your borrower? If the real estate market dips right when they anticipate putting it up for sale, would this property still rent for enough to bring in positive cash flow each month after monthly expenses are paid? Does the borrower have enough capital to make the desired exit strategy work?

Think of a borrower who wants to set up a short-term rental. Some properties are in strict homeowner's associations or municipalities that may limit short-term rentals or ban them altogether. In certain cities, for example, the borrower would need to apply for a license to run and operate a rental or use a licensed property management company. You are not going to know at the time of purchase whether the property or the borrower will be able to become permitted or licensed as a short-term rental, so discussing additional exit strategies with your prospective borrower will be critical.

Property Considerations to Contemplate
- Property purchase price, estimated rehab budget, and borrower capital contributions
- After-repair value or potential resale price
- Highest and best use of the property
- Average market rents (also known as pro forma rents)
- Land-use restrictions, including neighborhood covenants (homeowner's association restrictions), municipal, and/or zoning
- Environmental considerations such as flood zones, environmental hazards, and natural disaster impacts
- Utilities (septic versus sewer, well versus city water, etc.)
- Unique characteristics, including both good and bad traits about the property that could accelerate or limit the potential buyer pool (a view or shared access to a beach would be positive features while a single-family home surrounded by industrial properties or on a major arterial would be negative)

Property Valuation Note
Before you overevaluate the property during the Contact phase, realize that the value placed on the property will not be a specific number. If you have purchased your own home, you may have waited to receive the appraisal, which offered an exact figure. Know that an appraisal, while it may seem quite concrete, is merely an opinion of that appraiser as to the value of the property. You could hire a second appraiser to come out and do another appraisal and likely get a different number. At this stage of the lending opportunity, the ARV should be thought of more as a range than a number. There may be a lower-end number that reflects minimal updates and lower-quality finishes, a midrange value that represents typical amenities and finishes for the area, and then an upper range that reflects higher-end touches to the home or the inclusion of additional amenities that are in demand. Looking at the scope of work, you should be able to get an idea of the type of renovation the borrower is looking to do. You can also look at past projects the borrower has done and see what they elected to change out and update versus keep in each project. If you are worried about the potential value of the underlying asset for your loan, you can attach a lower limit valuation to the property and lower the amount of money you are willing to lend, effectively lowering your LTV.

The 70/30 Rule

In this step, you will need to crunch some numbers to see if they align with your lending criteria or not. There are a few metrics associated with a fix-and-flip that you will need to know how to calculate and/or verify if provided to you by the borrower. One of the standard rules of thumb for fix-and-flip projects is the 70/30 rule. Simply put, this means the total cost of the project—including acquisition costs, carrying costs, and rehab costs—is no greater than 70 percent of the total ARV. In other words, there should be a projected profit margin of 30 percent of ARV.

For illustrative purposes, say a borrower is purchasing a property for $250,000 and has a rehab budget of $75,000. He also estimates about $10,000 in carrying costs for a six-month hold while he completes a cosmetic rehab and a projected ARV of $500,000. The borrower will put down $60,000 and wants you to fund the remaining amount of $190,000 plus $75,000 rehab for a total loan amount of $265,000.

- Acquisition costs: $250,000
- Carrying costs: $10,000
- Rehab costs: $75,000
- **TOTAL PROJECT COSTS: $335,000/ARV $500,000 = 67%**

If everything goes as planned and the provided numbers are verified to be accurate estimates, this project should have a profit margin of 33 percent, which would meet the 70/30 rule. You are welcome to use whatever metric you feel most comfortable with, but this ratio is widely used by experienced and new flippers alike. You can read more about this industry standard on BiggerPockets.com under the Tools section. See the 70 percent rule.

BiggerPockets.com also has fix-and-flip calculators, primarily meant for investors to use when conducting deal analyses for new purchases. While this isn't exactly geared toward lenders, the same criteria used to underwrite a deal for a real estate investor can also be useful for the lender when doing a basic evaluation of a property's financials.

PAPERWORK

At the risk of sounding repetitive, we want to reiterate again that private lending is very dynamic and personal. Your lending terms and the borrowers you choose to work with can be quite different from someone else who is also doing private lending. While this freedom of choice is very attractive, it also means the practice of private lending is not black and white. There are a few rules you absolutely want to keep in place, and possibly even some documents you will require to fund a loan, but the rest is purely up to personal preferences and how you want your lending "business" to function. The aim of this chapter and the one that follows is not to have you collect everything we list but to identify which you personally deem necessary and provide you with the pertinent information to help you make an informed decision. One main advantage private lending has over other forms of real estate lending is its high level of flexibility. There are often fewer hoops to jump through when you are looking to close a loan with a borrower. Therefore, only ask for documentation that supports your ability to do the loan comfortably. Don't ask for information you are not able to decipher and that causes you confusion.

We also want to be clear: we are not saying to not collect *anything* from a potential borrower. If you ask for documentation, there should be a reason for asking. What are you hoping to learn from that documentation? Where are you going to find that information on the requested document? Asking for more documentation may not make the loan safer. Many new private lenders are tempted to simply run down the list and ask a potential borrower for everything. They believe doing so makes the loan a sure bet to be repaid. However, you will need to be selective in the documents you request and cater your list to only the information you need to help you determine how to move forward.

Here are some common items you may want to collect from the borrower at this step in the process. If the initial meeting and review of some or all of these documents reinforces your decision to fund this loan, you can proceed with the additional paperwork in the next step, Compile & Condition. Remember: This is like peeling layers off an onion.

Borrower Application

Also known in the conventional lending space as the Uniform Residential Loan Application, or Form 1003 – Fannie Mae, this is the standard form used by nearly all mortgage lenders in the United States. This basic form and its equivalent, Form 65 – Freddie Mac, is completed by borrowers when they apply for a mortgage loan. The form is comprehensive and requires the borrower to answer many of your fundamental questions related to the loan purpose and the borrower's employment history, assets and liabilities, net worth, etc. It creates an overall storyline about the borrower in a standardized format. You can do a web search for "Universal Loan Application 1003" to find blank, fillable PDF copies to use with your loan applicants.

Please be aware that this form requires the borrower to share sensitive information, and it is your duty, as the potential lender, to safeguard this information. Take special care in how you electronically receive documents like the borrower application, which could include personal contact information, sensitive financial information, and the borrower's Social Security number. We always suggest telling the borrower to exclude inputting their Social Security number on the form, as we do not intend to use this data. It is also important you know how to properly store or dispose of sensitive borrower data if provided to you in hard copy (paper) format. Be sure to have some proper systems in place for document receipt and retention. We will discuss information security in the next chapter.

Purchase and Sale Agreement (PSA) and Seller's Disclosures

This is the formal document to acquire the property. It outlines under what terms and time frame the sale is to happen. This legally binding contract must be signed by both the buyer and seller to be considered valid. Additionally, most (if not all) states require some form of disclosures by the seller. This indicates age and condition of the property, including any known repairs, maintenance, capital improvements, structural issues, leaks, and environmental issues such as lead and asbestos, among other things. If you are not familiar with what this form covers or what is required in your state, you will want to find out from a real estate attorney or a trusted real estate broker.

Be sure to familiarize yourself with what is required for a legally binding purchase and sale contract in your state. For example, in the state of Washington, a legal description must be included and initialed by both parties for it to be considered a valid transaction. Additionally, a closing agent must be identified as well. The agreement will also list the date that the buyer/borrower must close on the transaction. It is important for you to identify the closing deadline and determine whether you can achieve that date or not. If the closing date is five days away and you need longer to decide whether you are comfortable or not, you may choose to decline this opportunity and wait for one with a longer timeline.

Interior Pictures, Site Visit, or Video of Property

Images and video are helpful to quickly analyze if the renovations a borrower has planned are sufficient or if additional updates and costs might be needed. You can also physically walk through the property if you and the borrower are in close proximity to it. Another way to quickly check this information is by having a link to the property listing online.

Borrower Strategy Form

Remember that you're not lending to someone who will make the property their primary residence. They're looking to repair and resell the property at a profit or keep the property and refinance into a bank loan. You need to know they've done their homework and have created a business plan. One of the key questions, in fact, is whether the property will be owner-occupied; this may be relevant if there's a question about usury laws. Also, the form requires the borrower to write out their answers rather than check a box. If the borrower is explaining their intentions with a property in their own words, in their own handwriting, it is very hard to challenge that in court should something go wrong, such as the borrower moving into the subject property.

We will discuss the borrower strategy letter in greater detail later on, but the key elements to remember are the intended use of the property, how long the renovation will take and cost, a detailed explanation of the investment strategy, the anticipated exit strategy, and any other relevant information about the property and project that the borrower wishes to share.

Schedule of the Borrower's Real Estate Transactions or Project Experience

The more experience your borrower has, generally the lower the risk. It's possible you will be lending to someone who's doing this for the first time, so price and plan accordingly. A first-time investor may not know what they don't know, so they often pose a higher risk than a borrower with significantly more experience and a proven track record.

Schedule of Real Estate Owned

A schedule of real estate is simply a list of properties the borrower has invested in over the past several years and still owns. Some of your applicants will have no experience and hence no schedule of real estate, except perhaps their own primary residence. Other applicants will have many properties listed.

List of References

This can be rather informal, but we felt the need to include it as possible paperwork should you want to formalize the process. This is not part of the traditional loan application, so if you are planning to consistently collect this information, it may be best to make this a separate form that goes out to every new potential borrower. To handle this in a simpler way, you could have the borrower email you the name and contact information of their references and a brief description of how they know those individuals.

As mentioned earlier, having a phone conversation with a reference is preferred over an email exchange. This gives you a chance to immediately follow up with additional questions should you feel you need them to elaborate on some points. The objective of your conversations is to gauge the borrower's reputation as an investor within the market. In any given area, repeated real estate activity tends to be focused on a small group of people.

Loan Overview or Term Sheet

This is typically the last piece of paperwork for this step and one you prepare rather than request from the borrower. After you receive some basic information about the borrower, their intentions of the property, and the loan amount they are seeking, you can get a rough idea if you are willing and able to fund the loan in the timeline they need. We first introduced this information in the Calculate & Evaluate pre-step. As a recap, your loan rates and terms should include:

- Total loan amount.
- Vested borrower name(s) and personal guarantors.
- Lender fees, including origination points, if applicable.
- Annual interest rate.
- Monthly interest payment amount and terms.
- Length of loan.
- Late fees and other penalties.
- Other loan terms, including personal guaranty required, funds held back at closing, or other stipulations.

While these terms are not set in stone, giving the borrower something in writing, with the understanding that things could change due to new information coming to light during your investigation (also known as underwriting), can go a long way in establishing some trust between you and the borrower. We've provided a sample term sheet in the supplemental materials (www.biggerpockets.com/lendingbonus) so you can see how one is typically structured.

You do not need to be overly formal about it; you could outline it in an email rather than type up a formal document. However, if you wish to communicate your terms, you should always place them in writing in case you need to review them again with the borrower.

When you are thinking about setting loan terms to mitigate risk, you need to keep state usury laws in mind, as you always want to have a legal loan with defensible rates and terms. If the loan was ever challenged in court and found to be above the usury limit, there could be hefty fines, loss of interest income, or worse, total or partial forgiveness of debt. This is where having a knowledgeable lending attorney comes into play. They can offer guidance on rates and terms that are legal and potentially price in the risk factors you feel are present in the project.

Realize that this is just a preliminary high-level review of the borrower and the property. No terms are set in stone at this point, but you also want to be up front with your lending guidelines as early as possible, with the little information provided thus far. The last thing you want to do is change terms on the borrower a few days before a closing. You also don't want to go through the time commitment of reviewing a bunch of borrower documents only to realize the borrower wants rates well below what you can offer. Before providing a term sheet outlining what you can do for your prospective borrower, you can always ask questions about expectations on rates and terms, such as:

- What kind of rates and terms have you received on past projects (if they are experienced)?
- What rates and terms are you expecting for a loan like this?
- How long of a loan are you looking for?
- Are you willing to provide a personal guaranty for your loan and are your other partners willing to as well?

Regardless of your approach, make sure you and the borrower are in the same ballpark before moving forward with the tedious task of loan processing and underwriting. It will save you a lot of time if you find you are not, in fact, aligned.

RISKS AND REWARDS

In the Contact step, like the Connect step, risks are usually limited to the time spent talking to a borrower, collecting documentation, and reviewing that documentation. The process of meeting with prospective borrowers, gathering and reviewing a limited amount of documentation, and crunching some basic numbers on the project financials can be tedious and time-consuming. The tendency for time-sensitive individuals is to circumvent this process and handle as much as you can via emails. The borrower sends an email with a bunch of documents. You review by yourself and respond back. The borrower reviews your email, supplies more documents over email, then you review and respond back again.

While this may be the easier route in your mind, it's a good way to cheat yourself out of a learning opportunity. In the beginning, as you become more familiar with borrowers and their financing needs, you get a chance to learn more about real estate investing strategies as a whole. Each and every conversation you have with a potential borrower rewards you with key learnings—not just what you want to do as a lender but also what you do not want to do as a lender. Take the time needed to meet with your prospects in person and use the time to learn more about investing and to identify red flags and dealbreakers as well as best practices on what to look for in future deals. We have learned a ton from meeting with experienced investors, even if we did not end up funding their projects.

Another risk we will dive into in the next step is unauthorized individuals gaining access to personal information about your borrower. The borrower will be sending over some rather sensitive information and even discussing some sensitive topics over the phone or in a public place for a meeting. If, at any point, that information becomes compromised, and it can be proved you were the source of that breach, it can open you up to liability from the borrower. We will discuss some options for safeguarding their information in the next step of the loan process, but it bears mentioning here as a risk since you are likely going to be collecting a small subset of this paperwork in the Contact step before you begin officially processing and underwriting the loan.

While accumulating a lot of sensitive information about a stranger may not sound rewarding, this part of the loan process can be thrilling to some new lenders. This is often the part where they feel like real lenders. You might be filled with equal parts excitement and terror, especially if you have found someone you might want to work with as a potential borrower. As you begin this process, you are going to learn a lot in a short amount of time, and the first loan will be the steepest learning curve of all. Resist the temptation to get lost in analysis paralysis, but also learn to honor your gut feeling if a situation doesn't feel right. It can be extremely rewarding to come this far, learn about your market, your potential borrower, and their property and project, and realize what sort of returns you may be able to generate for yourself and your budding lending business. Keep in mind that there is still a long way to go and many details to figure out, but getting a lot of this basic information at this stage can and will make the process smoother. You are one step closer to potentially funding a loan, or at least one loan file smarter when it comes to why you may deny a lending opportunity. Either way, you win!

A Note about Usury Laws

Since you are defining your rates and terms in this step, it's important to discuss usury law and how that will impact your lending guidelines and practices. Usury is the act of lending money at an interest rate that is considered unreasonably high or that is higher than the rate permitted by law.

Usury laws set a limit on how much interest can be charged on a variety of loans, such as payday loans, credit cards, or personal loans. One of the chief goals of usury laws is the prevention of excessively high loan rates and fees by any sort of lender. They are intended to offer some protection against predatory lending, so understanding the usury laws in your chosen market will be important for you as a private lender.

In the United States, usury laws are mostly regulated and enforced by the states rather than the federal government. They therefore vary widely depending on the state where you are lending. To make things more complicated, if you live in one state and the borrower lives in another, with the property in a third state, it can get messy when deciding which state usury laws you must adhere to when drawing up the documents and setting loan terms. Most states will set a limit on the interest rates and fees according to the type of loan and purpose of that loan. This is one of the many reasons why you need to make it clear that this is a loan for an investment property and for business purposes. Loans for primary residences tend to have much lower thresholds for fees and interest rates and an increase in documentation required for the loan to be considered legal. Loans made for the improvement, construction, or purchase of investment real estate may be subject to a different maximum annual rate of interest over the life of the loan.

Usury doesn't apply to just the interest rate you are charging a borrower. Some states include any fees charged to the borrower as part of an annualized interest rate, even if that includes default interest payments or late fees. Other states look at just the performing interest rate of the loan to categorize whether or not the loan is within limits for usury.

Penalties for violating usury laws also vary by state. Depending on the severity of the case, the penalty may require the bank or lender to return all interest charged from the borrower. It can also include additional fees that can be double or triple the original interest charge as well as added assessment fees. Furthermore, the violations can cause the loan to be declared illegal and thus repayment by the borrower may not be necessary. To stay within these limits and comply with the laws, it is imperative that you work with an attorney familiar with lending in your market to inform you on the limits and requirements of certain types of loans.

The only way to be certain about the usury laws in your state is to check them online. This is a major reason we advocate getting an attorney familiar with lending in your area. Even reading the legal state statutes online can cause more confusion than provide answers.

Another side note related to usury: These laws do not govern the licensing requirements a lender may need in that state. This set of rules just deals with the terms of the loan.

LESSONS LEARNED

The Kalyan family came to Betty, an experienced private money lender, for a loan they needed in order to pull out $100,000 from their two duplexes. Betty reviewed their loan application and properties and decided the projected profit margins were too narrow to merit pulling equity out of their existing real estate portfolio. It was not just the $100,000 the Kalyans needed from her; it was also the additional loan they would be taking out on the property they wanted to fix-and-flip nearby. Normally Betty did not have an issue using the equity of a borrower's existing real estate portfolio to provide them with necessary funds to acquire new projects, but this deal felt especially tight, with projected margins only at 25 percent of total project costs, rather than the standard 30 percent she was used to lending on.

After a few back-and-forth emails and phone calls, the Kalyans finally convinced Betty to come visit them in person and walk their duplexes at the same time. Once there, Betty discovered a backstory that really touched her. The Kalyans were an immigrant family from India who came to the United States, to live out the American Dream. The father worked in the landscaping and general contracting business and had saved up to purchase both duplexes as rentals. He also rehabbed three of the four units they owned. His eldest son, Shakeel, helped his dad and learned how to replace flooring, tile bathrooms, and update kitchens. It was impressive and touching to Betty to hear Mr. and Mrs. Kalyan speak about being able to provide an opportunity for Shakeel to learn real estate investing and create an American Dream of his own. This loan request was really for Shakeel, not for the Kalyans.

Suddenly, Betty realized the projected profit margins of 25 percent of total project costs were a much bigger deal to Shakeel than they were for older, experienced flippers who may typically look for more healthy returns of 30 percent or more. He was only 20 years old and wanted to get his foot in the door with real estate investing, and his parents were willing and able to help support his goals financially, physically, and emotionally. Mr. Kalyan promised to assist his son with any labor support he needed to keep costs down, and both parents were willing to personally guarantee the loan. After meeting with the Kalyans and Shakeel, Betty decided to fund the loan. While the project took a few months longer than anticipated, Shakeel sold the property for 20 percent more than his projected ARV, paid off Betty, and made a healthy profit to pocket until he found his next deal.

If Betty had not taken the time to go and meet with the Kalyans in person, she would have missed out on learning about their experience in greater detail and their personal story and journey to the United States. More importantly, she would have missed out on providing an opportunity to a promising young man to prove that he could employ all the lessons he'd learned from his dad on a successful real estate investment.

CONTACT IN REVIEW

C	**CONTACT** In this step, the goal will be to make introductory contact with your identified prospective borrower to determine if you would want to proceed with this borrower and/or property given the project level and to establish preliminary rates and terms of the deal with that specific borrower.		
P	**PERSON** Have a follow-up call, Zoom, or in-person meeting with prospective borrower to learn more about their experience, current project, and borrowing needs. At this point, you may also ask for professional references so that you can have similar conversations with these people before diving into the actual loan process.	**PROPERTY** Depending on if the borrower has a current project to fund, you may need the property address, purchase price, pictures, project budget, and other high-level information to start out. This is the time to crunch some general numbers about the prospective loan and project to make sure it fits your established criteria. Depending on the situation, you may even want to meet at the current project site.	**PAPERWORK** Prior to providing your rates and terms on a prospective loan, you may want to review the following key pieces of paperwork: • Borrower Strategy Letter • References • Purchase and Sale Agreement • Loan overview application and term sheet (written overview of your loan offer)
R	**RISKS AND REWARDS** There aren't usually many risks associated with the Contact step. This is your chance to "pre-qualify" a borrower and their project to see if it'll be a good fit for you. The more thorough you are in this step, the less time you will waste collecting and reviewing additional documentation, especially if the borrower is under tight timelines to close a purchase. The risk relates to loss of time and any money you may have spent to collect these preliminary documents. The rewards are properly screening a potential lending opportunity, so you have a higher likelihood of funding a loan.		

CALL TO ACTION FOR CONTACT

After reading this chapter, you will need to:

1. Prepare for your first meeting with your prospective borrower by reviewing questions you want to ask during your conversations and conducting web searches on the person and/or entity.

2. Do a little online research about the property specifications in advance of the meeting if the borrower provided you with some information about themselves or the property.

3. Read up on the 70/30 rule on BiggerPockets.com and research other methods for evaluating fix-and-flip deals.

Chapter 6
COMPILE &
CONDITION

CALCULATE & EVALUATE > CONNECT > CONTACT > **COMPILE & CONDITION** > COMPOSE & CLOSE > COLLECT & CONVEY

COMPILE & CONDITION QUICK PEEK

C	**COMPILE & CONDITION** In this step, the goal is to receive and review all the necessary documents and information needed to underwrite and approve the loan for funding.

	PERSON	**PROPERTY**	**PAPERWORK**
P	The primary person involved in this step is the borrower, as they are responsible for providing documentation. Other people might be insurance brokers, escrow/closing agents, and professional references of the borrower.	Depending on the plan for the property, you will be verifying information related to the property, such as current condition, estimates for rehab, rental income, and value after renovations.	There is plenty of paperwork involved in this step! Here, you will need to verify documentation related to the borrower's character, capacity, capital, collateral, and conditions.

R	**RISKS AND REWARDS** This can be the riskiest part of the loan process. Failure to do proper and thorough due diligence could lead to greater risks and challenges after the loan is funded. The rule of thumb is to find any and every reason you could possibly say no to this deal and assess if there is a way to mitigate that no to a yes.

At this point, you have connected with prospective borrowers and other key contacts to reach out to on various aspects of your private lending adventures. After finding a prospective borrower through these networking opportunities, you set up an initial one-on-one meeting to discuss their current project and lending needs. If you have made the decision to proceed with the loan based on your limited contact, you will continue your analysis of the loan in this Compile & Condition step.

In this step of the loan, we will look at the process of collecting documents and further evaluating the borrower's ability to undertake the project given their experience, income levels, and capital available, among other variables. In the lending world, this is called "loan processing": the accumulation of information from the borrower about the borrower, their business entity, and the property itself. Once these are received, we perform what is called "loan underwriting," which is the act of "inspecting what we expect" and reviewing the documentation to substantiate what the borrower told us in both their loan application as well as in our discussions with them.

Large lenders traditionally have a clear distinction between gathering documents, known as processing the loan, and then evaluating those documents to be in accordance with the lending standards, known as underwriting. Those two processes are very different and usually done by separate individuals within the same company. In the case of a private lender—especially one just starting out—these two are often performed on an ongoing basis and by the same person: you. In general, you will receive documents and evaluate them as they come in. You may also ask for more documents to support or answer additional questions, known as loan conditions in the conventional lending world. More established lenders will not begin underwriting a loan file until all the documents have been received through the processing phase. We suggest looking at documents as they come in, as this affords the borrower the time they need to get any additional documentation you may want to help evaluate the lending opportunity. It also gives you—as a beginner—the extra time to review each document thoroughly and to ask for additional help from others, should you need it.

As we discuss the documents related to the borrower and the property as well as what to look for in those documents, you may wonder, "What is reasonable? What is not? And how will I know?" Reviewing documents and determining your standards and limitations will be a work in progress. We can provide you with some guidelines on what other lenders may consider, but it will ultimately be up to you to decide what seems best for your own risk tolerance and comfort levels. We suggest starting off on the more conservative side of things. Augment and adjust your parameters over time when you gain more experience and have a more grounded perspective from which to operate your lending practices.

Lending Is a Calculated Risk

When underwriting and performing due diligence, a key point to remember is this: You will never know everything. Making a loan always involves some risk and always has some unknown factors. If there were zero risk, everybody would be in the lending business, and interest rates would plummet from the added competition!

Champion poker player Annie Duke has written an excellent book, *Thinking in Bets: Making Smarter Decisions When You Don't Have All the Facts*, on the topic of making educated decisions based on the information available to you, with the full acceptance that some information may never be available. In her experience and expertise on behavioral-decision science and decision education, Duke writes:

> What good poker players and good decision-makers have in common is their comfort with the world being an uncertain and unpredictable place. They understand that they can almost never know exactly how something will turn out. They embrace that uncertainty and, instead of focusing on being sure, they try to figure out how unsure they are, making their best guess at the chances that different outcomes will occur. The accuracy of those guesses will depend on how much information they have and how experienced they are at making such guesses. This is part of the basis of all bets.

Good decision-makers strive to calculate the odds of success (in this case, the borrower being able to repay the loan in full) versus failure (the borrower defaulting and the necessity of foreclosure or other corrective action). Good underwriters (and lenders) are comfortable with uncertainty and accept the fact that they will never know everything about a particular loan situation. The goal is to determine the likelihood of a positive outcome over other possibilities, knowing that luck may play a role as well. Duke sums it up well with this: "Improving decision quality is about increasing our chances of good outcomes, not guaranteeing them."

Like playing poker, underwriting is more of an art than a science. No two loan requests, borrowers, or properties are ever the same. While certain success elements must always be present, there's no rigid template you can simply use to replicate one loan after another. We wish it was that easy! This can make learning how to effectively evaluate loans a very difficult and time-consuming process. Like any other skill, proficiency at loan underwriting increases with time and practice. This is one of the reasons why—especially when you're starting out—you must only lend money that you can afford to lose, erring on the side of caution and protection of principal, rather than chasing return on investment. Hopefully, you won't lose it and you'll make a profit, but the odds that you make a mistake and lend to the wrong person or on the wrong property will get lower as you become more experienced. When starting out, what matters is trying to figure out how to make minor mistakes and not costly ones based on quality decision-making.

Where to Place Your Bets

Some private lenders do not care to dig into the borrower very much, as they are more interested in the collateral securing their loan. If the numbers work out on the property, they do not care if the borrower defaults because they could recoup their capital investment through foreclosure or repossession of the property. Some call this lending approach "loan to own" lending. A word of warning on this line of thinking: Depending on where the property is located, it may take an extended period of time to liquidate the property to recoup your principal investment and any interest, penalties, or legal fees incurred. Foreclosure in some states can take months, while in other states it can take *years*. Therefore, while the idea of "just take the property back" is simple enough in theory, it can be much more complicated and time-consuming in practice. This is another area where a qualified attorney can help you navigate how to avoid foreclosure or make you aware of the timeline and requirements for foreclosure. Additionally, if you are really interested in taking back properties on defaulting loans, why wouldn't you just flip properties yourself? The goal with private lending should never be to take a property back.

On the flip side, there are lenders who care very much about the borrower and less about the property itself. Their belief is that it's not the property doing the work; the person operates the property and makes decisions for the property. While both the person and the property are important, this debate is pertinent to new lenders. As you pursue private lending more and more, you will develop your own way of doing things and establish certain personal philosophies based on experience and your market. Do not fall into the rabbit hole of deeply investigating one without investigating the other. Instead, strive to know as much as you can about both the person(s) and the property in order to make the most informed and calculated decision possible. You can do all the due diligence on a borrower you want, but if they fall off their roof cleaning the gutters two days after closing, the property (and equity buffer in the property) is what will pay back the debt if the borrower fails to perform on the loan.

Now that we've discussed the intended goals of the Compile & Condition step, we will walk you through all the key considerations and documentation you may need to effectively decide whether to fund the loan or not. Keep in mind that this is a document-heavy section. We will cover a lot of paperwork related to both the borrower and the property. The intention is not to request things you cannot understand or which you may not care about. Rather, we will cover standard documentation requests and how you should interpret each of them. This will give you more insight into which pieces you may weigh more heavily than others, which ones you may choose to leave out altogether, and which ones are going to be required documents on every deal moving forward.

While it may seem like a lot, we are only scratching the surface regarding the documents to consider. There are simply too many datapoints involved in each piece of paperwork to cover in a single book. We will give you the type of document to request, what data you should be looking for, and why it could be important. In the interest of being able to reference things easily and quickly later on, we have created three thorough "Underwriting Deep Dive" chapters in the third part of this book. If you are looking for additional details about documentation, what specifically to look for, and how to evaluate the risk from those details in a loan scenario, you can skip to this section.

At this stage, you are trying to establish proof through documentation that the potential borrower has the key qualities you're looking for. Often this focuses on evaluating the past performance of the borrower as well as their current personal financial health, which is necessary to close the loan, make payments, and pay the loan in full upon completion. In the finance world, these datapoints are often categorized as character, capacity, capital, collateral, and conditions. The first three are specifically related to the borrower, while collateral and conditions are related to the property and project.

Character
- **Overview:** Focuses on the borrower's trustworthiness, personality, and credibility
- **Objective:** To evaluate the borrower's past performance and future likelihood to fulfill financial obligations
- **Typical sources of documentation:** Credit report, credit score, professional references, relevant past experience, and background check

Capacity

- **Overview:** Focuses on the borrower's available cash flow and overall ability to repay a loan
- **Objective:** To evaluate the borrower's current cash position, overall assets and liabilities, and sources of income
- **Typical sources of documentation:** Personal financial statement, schedule of real estate, rental property Profit and Loss Statement (P&L), pay stubs, W-2s or other proof of employment and salary, and tax returns

Capital

- **Overview:** Focuses on the borrower's capital contributions toward a property or project
- **Objective:** To determine if the borrower has sufficient cash reserves necessary for a down payment, rehab costs, and contingencies, as well as minimum reserves potentially required for a refinance (a more common lender requirement since the pandemic)
- **Typical sources of documentation:** Bank statements, trade account statements, retirement account statements, and other sources of liquid assets

Collateral

- **Overview:** Focuses on the borrower's property or properties being used as collateral to secure the loan
- **Objective:** To determine if the borrower has a realistic and sufficient business plan to exit the project and repay the loan as well as reasonable equity protection to recover any principal and interest, should the loan default.
- **Typical sources of documentation:** Mortgage statements (for existing real estate owned), property valuation estimates and recent comps in area, schedule of real estate, title commitment, and hazard insurance policy quote

Conditions

- **Overview:** Focuses on the other conditions outside the borrower's control that may affect overall loan performance, such as the health of the real estate market and economy and the specifics of the loan
- **Objective:** To determine if other factors could adversely affect the project and property success and to also evaluate the loan amount, interest rate, intended use of funds, and other stipulations that may be needed to further secure the loan

- **Typical sources of documentation:** Real estate and economy news and trends, Borrower Strategy letter, project pro forma, contractor bids, rehab budget, project schedule, municipal planning, and development requirements

PERSON

During the Compile & Condition step, the prospective borrower does most of the work to gather the documentation you request of them. You, as the lender, are taking action to review the documents and request additional follow-up materials to further substantiate the borrower, should you need them. Remember, you may not need all these documents or require them for every loan. More documents don't necessarily make the loan safer. Knowing what to request as well as what not to request is important but knowing how to synthesize the data you receive is crucial.

This step will also include getting documentation from other involved parties, including a title commitment from the title company and insurance quotes from the borrower's insurance agent so you can review them for adequate coverage. You may also want to collect information from credit bureaus to evaluate the borrower's creditworthiness. Mostly, though, the borrower is central to completing this step.

Do not be surprised if borrowers are slow to respond, go "dark" on you for days at a time, or send you the wrong documents. This is fairly common, as most flippers wear multiple hats and are pulled in a number of different directions. Some lenders won't work with borrowers who are not responsive enough, and we totally understand this stance. We typically extend a little grace since, in our experience, many flippers are juggling multiple responsibilities and projects. It will be up to you to determine how problematic this lack of communication is.

The documentation outlined below is being requested from the borrower with the assumption that the documents you received in the Contact step have been reviewed and adequately meet initial lending guidelines to proceed. Now the goal is to analyze more documents to substantiate answers provided to you earlier. As another lender colleague first told us when starting out, "Assume everyone's lying to you." It sounds so jaded but the point is just because they tell you one thing does not mean you take that as the truth. Ask for proof, verified by a third party. For example, if the borrower tells you they make $100,000 at a tech job, get a pay stub or two. A healthy dose of doubt will protect you in the long run.

If you use the 1003 universal loan application we recommended in the Contact step, it asks for information such as asset levels, the types of assets held, the income of the borrower, and other properties the borrower may own. Many of the documents you will request from the borrower verify information the borrower provided on their loan application. Certain details may not need to be verified if you are not as concerned about them. For example, if your borrower is an experienced fix-and-flip investor, the borrower may not have any additional properties other than their primary home listed under the Assets or Real Estate Owned section of the application. In this case, it might be better to ask for a project experience spreadsheet, similar to a schedule of real estate, which details the properties the borrower has previously owned. This will allow you to search each one in online public records to see how the title was held and how long they owned the property. Again, not every loan is going to require every single document listed in this book. Use your best judgment to determine what may be necessary and reach out to ask for help when you are unsure.

Verification of Identification

Photo ID

This sounds so simple, but it is often overlooked. Ask for a copy of a government-issued identification card that shows their current address of their primary residence. This also verifies that the person you met with for coffee is actually the borrower they say they are on their application and other documentation related to the loan. Obtain a copy of identification from all borrowers who are listed on the Purchase and Sale Agreement.

Business-Entity Documents

You may be lending to a business entity that will be the vested owner of record on the title. This is common with real estate investors and another way of ensuring your loan is business in nature. In fact, many private money experts will only lend to business entities for this reason. It is a much harder case to make that the loan was for personal or consumer use when it was made to a business. If you lend to a business entity, you need to see the required legal instruments related to the entity formation. There are different compulsory documents depending on how the business is set up.

- **Sole proprietorship, partnership, or limited liability corporation (LLC):** You will need to collect an Operating Agreement and the Certificate of Formation. The name of the document might be different based on the state in which the business was formed, but it should identify the partners of the business, the percentage of ownership in the business for each partner, which partner has the power to sign loan documents and take out credit in the name of the business, and other agreements between members.

- **Corporation (typically a S-corp or C-corp designation with the state and IRS):** You will need to collect the Articles of Incorporation and the Certificate of Formation. The Certificate of Formation is similar to the Operating Agreement but generally more complex, as it outlines the specific nature of the business.

While there are many similarities between the two documents, the key difference is the Operating Agreement defines how the entity conducts business internally, while the Articles of Incorporation define how the entity conducts business within the state. When in doubt on what documentation to collect, ask your trusted real estate attorney.

A word of warning about business entities needs to be shared here. Just because a borrower has gone through the steps to create a business legally does not mean it is a "legitimate" business with revenue, assets, and profits. Most states allow anyone to open a business entity online with some simple forms and a few hundred dollars of fees. Do not get lulled into a false sense of security just because a borrower has a business or multiple business entities.

Character, Credit, and Capacity

As mentioned in the Contact step, you will use your first conversations and the follow-up activity of calling down on professional references to confirm trustworthiness and character. If you chose to wait until after loan terms were mutually agreed upon, now would be the time to make those calls to references provided by the borrower.

Here are a few additional items to check related to credit and capacity.

Credit History

This may or may not be important or relevant to you as a lender. While you can set up credit check services through vendors such as the credit bureaus themselves, this can create additional steps and disclosures as well as added costs. In accordance with the Fair Credit Reporting Act, you are required by law to request authorization in writing from all borrowers prior to running a credit report. You may need to explain to the credit-check vendor why you need access to this information or you may need to set up a business entity for your lending. You might not be interested in the score number per se but getting an idea of the borrower's payment history and debt level may also be of interest to you as the lender.

Alternatively, you can have the borrower run a free credit report online and share it with you. This takes the burden off of you, saves you on costs, and simplifies the process. Tools such as the website www.freecreditreport.com can be suggested to a borrower. While it won't provide a credit score, it will list out the borrower's liabilities and payment history. If you are keen on knowing the borrower's credit score, there are institutions and credit card companies, such as Bank of America, that offer those free to consumers, as well as other banks and credit unions, including American Express, Ally Bank, and Citi Bank. Discover Credit Scorecard offers this service free whether you are cardholder or not.

Here are some red flags to look out for on any credit report you receive.
- Too many revolving accounts with high balances
- High volume of late payments
- Too many mortgages with high loan-to-values
- Credit lines that are near their maximum allowable balances
- Expensive vehicles with large balances owed

It will be up to you to decide what you are comfortable with accepting.

Capital Resources
You may want to determine how much cash your borrower can access. This is known as liquid assets. The borrower will disclose their asset levels on the loan application, so you are simply verifying that those accounts are active and the estimated amounts match the amounts on the statements. Realize that liquid accounts may change in value over time, especially accounts made up of equities like stocks. You mostly want to establish the amount of capital your borrower has access to in order to perform on the loan, including any down payment and closing costs that must be paid to close on the property.

Types of account statements to potentially review include:
- Personal and/or business bank depository accounts (both checking and savings).
- Open, unused HELOCs.
- Brokerage trade accounts, stocks, index funds, etc.
- Certificates of deposits (CD).
- Cash-value life insurance.
- Retirement accounts (401(k), SEP, IRA, etc.).

Here's what to look for when reviewing these capital resources.
- Is the statement current and most recent?
- Is the name on the account the same as the borrower?
- Do the stated capital amounts on the loan application match the respective statement amounts?

Proof-of-Funds Statements

The borrower may be receiving funds from unsecured business loans that do not appear on their credit reports. What you want to avoid is a borrower that has taken on a considerable amount of debt to make their asset account levels increase artificially. If these unsecured loans are not being reported to the personal credit report of your borrower and are not secured against real estate, you will have no way to know if the assets you think are there are in fact liabilities. You can ask for a proof-of-funds statement from the borrower to explain where large deposits come from or to acknowledge that there are no outstanding liabilities against them or the business to which they are personally liable for repayment.

Cash Flow and Income Sources

Income and Employment Verification

Beware of information overload in this category. It is a common misconception for new lenders to assume they should request and review tax returns. Not only is this a very sensitive piece of information, but it almost always has *too* many datapoints in it to make it really worthwhile to review as a beginner.

Conventional bank lenders generally want to see one or two years of the borrower's tax returns and you may feel it is necessary to review income if the borrower is commission-based or self-employed. A borrower may be reluctant to release such personal information to a total stranger, and you may feel reticent to ask for something so detailed and sensitive. Therefore, have a good idea of what you want to see on these tax returns. You can also ask specifically for certain parts of the tax return such as the Schedule E, which provides information about rental property income. Personally, we do not typically ask for these documents in our current lending businesses and, instead, ask for pay stubs and W-2s, 1099-MISCs, or business and/or rental P&Ls acknowledged by the borrower's certified public accountant (CPA). This can provide similar information without the headache of having to sift through personal tax returns.

Other Business Entities or Ownership

You will also want to know (to the extent possible) if the borrower has other businesses and if those businesses are in good standing. Some active investors will set up multiple LLCs, for example, with possibly one LLC per property they own. Others will set up a different LLC for each partnership they are a member of, as they may own different real estate assets with different partners in different parts of the country. Verification of business entities can be done easily through government agency websites such as the secretary of state's. Some lenders may not choose to verify other business entities that the borrower is a member of unless that is a source of income identified on their borrower application.

PROPERTY

While this step is very heavy on documentation, there are some items that are related to the property as well as some considerations specifically about the property itself.

The amount of paperwork related to the property or properties being used to secure the loan can be a long list and will depend on (a) the type of work being done, (b) who will be involved in the project, and (c) other factors such as if you are lending on renovations being done.

Property Valuation

There are a few options to determine the value of the property as well as a few different values you can assign to a property. As we mentioned in the Contact stage, you will want someone in your network to do a property valuation. The property (and the equity available) is the backstop for loss of money in your loan. Determining the value of that asset (both current as-is value as well as after-repair value) is probably one of the most important aspects of the property to establish. When pre-qualifying a deal in the Contact step, you likely came up with ballpark numbers or the borrower supplied some for you. Now is the time to validate a more detailed valuation of the property in question.

Realize that the value is more of a range than a single target number. It can also change from one analysis to another. You can use a full appraisal, get a broker price opinion or a comparative market analysis done, or use an online value service vendor. Each have their own benefits and downsides, which are discussed at length in Chapter Ten. Generally, the lender creates or orders the valuation report, and—depending on the method—either requests the borrower remit payment directly to the service provider (typical for full appraisals, which cost more) or fronts the payment themselves (for BPOs and CMAs) and charges back the borrower at close.

Project Pro Forma or Deal-Analysis Sheet

Every investor should have this completed for you to review. It details the entire project financials in a single sheet (or two) for a quick high-level overview of the capital coming in and the capital going out. It will allow you to validate the purchase price, the monthly carrying costs, including interest payments (if any), monthly insurance premiums, utilities, and property taxes. It will also include financing costs such as points and other lender fees, as well as fees associated with selling the property once completed. These are called "closing costs" and will include real estate agent commissions, excise taxes, and other closing charges associated with title and escrow. The project pro forma will also have a high-level rehab budget. All this will be listed to give you (and the borrower) an idea of projected profit margins, should everything go as planned.

Rehab Budget, Scope of Work, and/or Contractor Bids

These documents outline the operational details of the business plan. You need to see solid (and realistic) numbers to back up the borrower's business plan and exit strategy. You should see line-by-line details for each area of the renovation. Ask vendors in your market about rough estimates for repairs listed on the scope of work if you are unsure. Compare the list of repairs and replacements with photos or videos provided by the borrower. If you were able to walk the property with the borrower, refer to any notes you made during that visit. Also take into consideration the scope of work for the exit strategy the borrower is wanting to pursue. For example, if the scope of work lists out putting high-end finishes into a property that is slated to be a rental, they may be over-improving the property.

If you ever have questions, reach out to investors you met in in the Connect step or have a contractor walk the property with you while going over the scope of work. This is an area where having an experienced borrower can really lighten the load on you as a lender. Experienced investors tend to have committed crews, stockpiles of supplies, and a system of tackling projects that produces a solid renovation in a streamlined timeline—and often for less capital due to scales of economy.

Hazard Property Insurance Policy and Binder

This type of insurance physically covers the property should the structure be damaged by a covered event. The hazard insurance falls on the borrower to obtain. They should provide you with a copy of the declaration page and a copy of the policy for you to review. It is important for you to ensure the borrower has secured proper and appropriate levels of insurance coverage in case of damage or destruction. Another reason property insurance is important is that you, as the lender, will need to be insured as a mortgagee or loss payee on the insurance policy. This will ensure you are paid out first on a policy claim before the borrower is paid out.

Intentionally or not, the borrower will likely try to find the least expensive insurance rates for the property, and a broker can tweak many different variables to get the lowest premium possible. This can leave gaps in coverage or result in insufficient coverage in the event of an incident at the property. Additionally, depending on the property and its intended use, you will need different types of coverage. For example, if the property will be vacant during rehab, you will want coverage for vandalism and theft. You as the lender just need to make sure you are protected should something happen to the property, which is why you need to review the insurance documents before closing. We will cover some additional ins and outs to watch for with regards to property insurance in the underwriting chapters of this book.

Flood Insurance

This may not be required for every property. It largely depends on the flood zone assigned to the property according to Federal Emergency Management Association (FEMA) flood maps. There are a few different things to recognize about flood insurance. First, the FEMA flood maps can and do periodically get updated and redrawn. While the property may not be in a flood zone, there is no assurance it will remain in that flood zone classification. The important thing is to check a FEMA flood zone map online to verify whether the property should require flood insurance or not. If in doubt, ask for help from an insurance agent you already work with and have them tell you their professional opinion. Flood insurance rates are expensive, much more so than typical hazard insurance, so make sure it is a necessity for the property, as you will likely get some pushback from your borrower if it is not.

PAPERWORK

When talking about lending on a cosmetic fix-and-flip project, where the borrower purchases the property, rehabs it, and then puts it back on the market, there are several key documents to review and evaluate before doing anything else. Making sure these documents are legally binding, thorough, accurate, and clear of any major red flags or roadblocks is essential before moving on to the laborious task of reviewing a bunch of borrower-provided documentation. After all, would you want to waste hours or days reviewing documents only to find out the purchase wasn't legally binding because it didn't have the seller signature on it and the seller ended up backing out? We wouldn't want that either, so let's first walk through the documents required for any purchase of an investment property, specifically the purchase and sale contract, any other legally binding documents required for the purchase, and the preliminary title report.

Reviewing Purchase Agreements

Purchasing a property can take place in several different ways. You can:

- Purchase a property using an agent or acting as the agent, off the multiple listing service (MLS). The MLS is how properties are actively bought and sold in the real estate market.
- Purchase a property not currently on the market (also known as off-market) directly from the seller (typically for sale by owner or without agent representation).
- Purchase an investment property through a wholesaler. This is when you purchase from a person who already has the property under contract and who will sell you their rights to the purchase contract.

In the first scenario, standardized residential Purchase and Sale Agreement forms are typically used. These are the easiest to read, as they are boilerplate templates that cover all the mandatory information (required data will vary by state) and any additional addenda, which may be needed to support a variety of special circumstances. What is nice about purchases listed on the MLS is that title and escrow are typically already opened with a seller-selected title and escrow company, so the preliminary title commitment will already be available to you. Additionally, since the contracts are established by the MLS using best practices and standardized formatting, you will be able to learn how to read the contracts easily after just a little experience.

In contrast, properties sold off-market through wholesalers or by owner may not have access to the MLS and, therefore, may use a nonstandardized purchase and sale contract. These contracts can vary widely, so it can be time-consuming to locate all the pertinent datapoints required to ensure that it's a legally binding contract and that it represents the interests of the buyer adequately. Finally, properties purchased through a wholesaler—which are common among real estate investors—require supplementary documents to guarantee they're a legally binding purchase between the wholesaler and the borrower. More on this in a bit.

Components to Review on a Purchase Contract

- **Who is listed as the buyer?** Is it the individual(s) you have been speaking to already or are there additional names or a business entity listed instead? If there are other buyers on this line with whom you have not yet had contact, request contact information and marital status for each of the individuals listed and ask for an explanation of each relationship. In a wholesale situation, the buyer will be the wholesaler and not your borrower. We discuss this scenario in more detail shortly.
- **What if the buyer is a business entity?** You will need to make note that the borrower will need to supply you with business-entity documents. All your loan documents will be created under this business entity as the maker of the loan. You will also need a personal guaranty. For information on how to review business-entity documents, see Chapter Nine: "Underwriting Deep Dive—Person."
- **Is the contract signed around by all parties?** This is critical. If only one party has signed, it is not considered "mutual" and there is no legally binding agreement to purchase. Make sure you obtain the final signed around contract if you have not yet received it. You may also wish to hold off on reviewing the loan if you feel your borrower does not have a strong likelihood of getting it under contract.
- **Does the purchase contract contain the necessary information to make it legally binding?** This may vary by state, but all purchase and sale contracts should have some or all of the following information:
  - Legal description and property tax parcel number attached, possibly initialed by all parties
  - Escrow closing office identified
  - Closing date listed
  - Signatures by both buyer(s) and seller(s)
  - Earnest money deposit—both a dollar amount and how it will be tendered (check, wire, or promissory note)

Other Things to Look Out For

- Has earnest money already been deposited with escrow?
- Who is responsible for paying closing costs, including commissions, title, and escrow?

- What contingencies are included and what are those timelines?
- Has the buyer waived any contingencies such as inspections, appraisal, or financing?
- Is there any seller financing associated with this purchase? If yes, what lien position is the seller expecting? (Seller held first would mean your loan would be in a second lien position.)

Purchases from Wholesalers

The transaction for a property being wholesaled to your borrower is a lot more complicated than a purchase off the MLS, for many reasons. First, since wholesalers are not always licensed real estate agents, they may not be using standardized forms, which makes it difficult to read the contracts provided to you. Second, the buyer on record will be the wholesaler, so an additional contract is needed to assign the rights to purchase the property over to the borrower. This is called an Assignment Agreement. Unless you are familiar with off-market real estate transactions, we suggest you proceed with caution and seek out support from your local real estate attorney or a real estate agent who may be more knowledgeable on the subject and can help review the contracts on your behalf.

In general, assigned contracts have more risk because there are additional parties involved. Also, properties being assigned will have hefty assignment fees attached to the transaction. While the deal may still pencil out handsomely despite the assignment fee, sometimes sellers can become disgruntled or back out altogether if the wholesaler does not handle the transaction and communication between parties well. You should not be afraid to lend on a wholesale deal, but there are extra complications and more paperwork involved so you should proceed with care.

Here are a few potential things to look out for.

- **Does the purchase contract list give the wholesaler the right to assign their rights to purchase the property?** Typically, this can be done with "and/or Assigns" after the wholesaler's name on the buyer line (e.g., "John Doe and/or Assigns"). If not, then the wholesaler may not be legally allowed to assign over their rights to your borrower.
- **Is there a valid Assignment Agreement created between the wholesaler and your borrower?** This is a separate document outlining the transfer of rights to purchase the property from the wholesaler. It lists out the parties included. This is where you can find your borrower name(s) or entity as the purchaser/buyer.

- **Does the seller require notice to change the name of the end buyer?** If not expressly written into the contract, even if there is an "and/or Assigns", the contract will need an addendum changing the buyer from the wholesaler to your borrower. This addendum will require sign-off from the seller. If the seller is unaware of a change in buyers up to this point, they may refuse to sign the addendum.
- **What are the expected terms of the assignment transaction?** There are several ways to handle an assignment. One was mentioned above, with a change in buyer using an addendum. If the seller is unwilling to sign the addendum, then other options will need to be entertained and subsequent contracts drawn up. Be sure to learn how this transaction will be taking place.
- **How much is the assignment fee and how will it be tendered?** Make note of the assignment fee and what percentage it is of the total purchase price. This will be important to include in the total project pro forma.
- **What are the terms to provide the assignment fee and did the borrower tender payment on the assignment fee yet?** You will need to locate in the contract when and to whom the assignment fee should be sent. Hopefully, for the borrower's sake, the assignment fee is to be tendered directly to the escrow closing company and not the wholesaler directly.

Should you have any questions you can't answer through your personal review of the purchase documents provided to you, you have resources available to you for assistance and guidance. You can:
- Request that your local real estate attorney review the Purchase and Sale Agreement and any supplemental contracts, including an Assignment Agreement.
- Contact your local title company and ask them if the purchase and sale transaction has been reviewed and approved to open escrow. They will usually not allow for escrow to be opened if the contracts furnished to them are incomplete. Just be aware that sometimes things can be missed by title and escrow—not out of incompetency but because of high transaction volumes—so do your own homework on the contracts as well.
- Check out the resources at www.biggerpockets.com/lendingbonus for additional firms and associations you could reach out to for support or a second opinion.

Assignment Fees

The saying "size matters" may or may not be true with assignment fees. We have seen six-figure assignment fees and yet the deal still pencils out. This is definitely a unicorn situation, but these types of deals are out there. Assignment fees typically range from a few thousand dollars to a sizable six-figure chunk, depending on the size of the deal. There are a few considerations you will need to make note of before moving forward.

First, how much is too much? While we can't answer this question for you, we can offer a couple points of view. One is our general rule of thumb that "a deal is a deal." Period. If the project can still have a potentially large profit margin even with a $25,000 assignment fee, then who cares? However, another school of thought comes from traditional hard-money lenders, who often cap assignments to a percentage of the total purchase price. This could be around 10 to 20 percent. Since the wholesaler performs many similar activities as a real estate agent who typically gets 1 to 4 percent of the contract price, this seems commensurate for the work the wholesaler completes to get the property under contract, often at below-market prices. This last point is what justifies the higher compensation. If the wholesaler can lock in a contract price much lower than market value, then the assignment fee will typically be inclusive of a share in that "instant equity."

Another concern is around fairness to the seller. Is the seller older and potentially at risk for elder abuse? This will be difficult to make a case around since you are a removed, indirect party to this transaction, but it is something to think about, both ethically and legally. Even if you have no moral opinions here, the legality of it could bring the transaction to a screeching halt if flagged by a concerned family member, the escrow company, or by the seller directly after discovering their "buyer" was actually selling to another end buyer for a huge profit. We have had circumstances where escrow companies refuse to close any deals with assignment contracts. For more rationale behind this, you should consult your local title officer and ask about their policy and what potential concerns to look out for on future deals.

The last concern is around fraud. While not all wholesale deals are fraud, this practice is less regulated and monitored than transactions completed by licensed real estate agents. Because of this, some wholesalers may straddle the line of ethical and responsible wholesaling. Daisy-chaining deals is one of those questionable practices. This happens when an individual tries to wholesale a deal that they do not have authority to sell. This wholesaler may just be trying to add another small assignment fee on top of the deal, payable directly to the whole-saler, in order to scam the end buyer, your borrower, out of a few thousand bucks.

While these issues are more of the borrower's responsibility to heed, as the potential lender, you still need to know all the legally binding and material participants on a real estate transaction under your consideration. It can be difficult to make sure the entire process is handled aboveboard so that you do not waste time and money on a deal that eventually falls through.

Preliminary Title Report

Once you have reviewed all documents related to the purchase of a property and deemed it a legally binding and mutual contract, you can move on to ordering and reviewing the preliminary title commitment on the property, also known as a title report. If it was already ordered by the listing agent, which is common on properties bought off the MLS, then you simply need to request this to be sent to you. You can call the title and escrow company listed directly on the purchase contract. However, if this is a situation where the investor will be purchasing a property off-market, then title is likely not opened and could take several days or longer to be returned to you.

While some lenders request the borrower to open up the title, we prefer to open it ourselves. The borrower has a lot of documents to gather up and if you can speed up the process by ordering a title commitment yourself, it will save a lot of time and give you the opportunity to review the title commitment as soon as it's ready. It also gives you the chance, as the lender, to order the proper Lender's Title Policy as well.

We could write more than one chapter about title reports, including title report issues (known as exceptions), how to "clear title," and what different title policies are needed for various real estate transactions. You can find several expert resources online to educate yourself about what title insurance is and what it isn't. If you want more background information about title insurance, we suggest heading to Chapter Eleven: "Underwriting Deep Dive—Paperwork," where we discuss terms related to titles in more depth. You can also go to the internet for some support or contact your title office and ask for any suggested resources. Our favorite local title company, Rainier Title and Escrow—a subsidiary of Stewart Title—has some great reference materials available online, which explain everything from the difference between title insurance policies, to red flags on title reports to be aware of, to a detailed overview of the escrow process. You might be surprised how helpful your local title representative can be in your learning process.

However, for the purposes of this book and to teach you how to protect yourself as a private lender, we will cover the bare basics of what you need to do to get a clean title report and order a Lender's Title Policy. At the end of the day, the title department where you open up the title, including the title officers on staff, will be your go-to resource for any detailed questions you may have regarding the property you are using to secure your loan.

What is a Title Commitment or Report?

A title company does research through public records to make sure a property owner can legally sell a piece of real estate to the buyer (your potential borrower). The title officer will determine who officially owns the home (also known as the vested owner) and whether the property has encumbrances against it. Encumbrances are liabilities associated with the property, such as mortgages or deeds of trust, personal or business judgments, or unpaid tax liens, etc. Some are voluntary such as mortgages, and some are involuntary such as judgments recorded against the owner in court, which are involuntarily placed on the property record. The results of this search are put together in a systematic way known as a title report.

Why Is a Title Report Important and What Am I Looking For?

Title reports show you who will be vested on the title as the new owner (your borrower). The title department doesn't just look at public records associated with the seller and the property; they also conduct searches on your borrower. If the borrower has a common name (like Johnson), they may request additional personal information from the borrower in order to clear their identity. This is called a "BID," or "borrower identification." For some of our borrowers, once they completed this process, personal liens and judgments were added on the title, such as IRS tax liens, personal judgments from lawsuits, and back child support from child services agencies. This is an important step to complete since the borrower needs to satisfy these liens before they are able to proceed with the transaction. In some instances, these issues on title, also known as special exceptions, can be a high dollar amount that the borrower is incapable of paying to remove the issue. If this is the case, the deal may need to be cancelled due to lack of liquidity. This is why ordering a title report is an extremely important step to complete as the lender.

How Do I Request a Lender's Title Policy?

You will request an ALTA Extended Lender's Policy in the name you wish to use as the lender—whether this is you as an individual or you and your spouse as a married couple or through a business entity. You will also want to order the policy in an amount at least equal to the loan amount, if not more. Some private lending attorneys recommend policies for 125 percent of the loan amount to cover any unforeseen issues with the loan that may require you to make a policy claim. We discuss this in greater detail in the resources at www.biggerpockets.com/lendingbonus.

How Do I Clear the Title Report?

We suggest you make this the job of the borrower and the title department. They are the experts and you working to clear any exceptions just makes you the middleman. If the title commitment has some exceptions that should be cleared, like the BID or liens and judgments, just forward the title report to your borrower and ask them to work directly with the title department.

If you have any questions about specific parts of the title report, ask your real estate attorney to review on your behalf and share with you their concerns. Early on when we were first starting out in private lending, our attorney offered to order the title report for us and to review it when it was returned to us. He was invaluable in helping us learn what special exceptions mattered and which ones did not. He also helped advise us on if and/or how to proceed based on the preliminary title report.

If everything checks out, the title company issues title insurance for that property at the time the loan is closed and funded. There are two types of title insurance: lender's title insurance and borrower's title insurance (also known as an owner's policy). Both are usually paid for by the borrower. Title insurance is crucial so a lender has assurances that the borrower has the lawful right to own that property and that there are no other liens on the property that may precede your loan in priority at the time of closing.

If you want to know more about how to read and clear title commitments, check out Chapter Eleven: "Underwriting Deep Dive—Paperwork." Finally, if you are not familiar with the typical title insurance and escrow closing costs in both identity and amount, now would be a great time to learn about that process. Realize that some fees will be standard, no matter what title company or closing attorney is used. These include document recording fees, rates to transfer the deed in the form of deed stamps, and other municipal-related fees. Some states also have mortgage stamps, which are fees based on the loan amount. As you can see, there are going to be a lot of fees associated with closing the loan for both the buyer (your borrower) and the seller. The good news is most are paid by those two parties in a typical transaction. The title insurance policy costs can typically be found on the first page of the title commitment while escrow closing fees are typically found on the escrow closer's rate sheet and on their website.

There is a lot more paperwork you *could* ask for during this phase. However, in order to keep the process moving along, we suggest you create a baseline of required documents from the borrower (or a third party, if applicable) and only ask for additional supplemental documents if you feel you need more details to clear a specific area of the five C's of credit. In underwriting, the act of creating additional loan requirements is called "loan conditions." After reviewing the standard required documentation, an underwriter may ask for supplemental information before clearing the loan to close.

For example, if the borrower shows you a rehab budget with a line item for windows at only $5,000 for the entire project and you believe it should be at least double that amount, you may wish to ask for the window bid to review. Or if you review the borrower's bank statements and notice a large deposit that will be used for down payment, you may want an explanation for where those funds came from. Did they earn it on a previous project or was it gift money? An explanation letter may help address any concerns you have about the source of those funds.

Check out the supplemental materials at www.biggerpockets.com/lending bonus for a list of minimum required documents from each author's perspective. While one of us prefers to do a detailed review of the borrower's personal financials and previous project experience, the other tends to place more weight on the property equity and project financials. Each of us will provide our sample set of initial documents that we collect and the rationale to support our decisions. We've also created a required-documents checklist, where you can customize which documents you want to collect for each loan request and assign owners and due dates. This will help you keep track of what is coming in, what documents have been cleared and are satisfactory, and what other documents or requirements you may still need in addition to what has been provided.

Safe, Secure Transmittal and Storage of Borrower Documentation

This is the perfect opportunity to remind you again about how to collect paperwork and maintain it safely. Many of these documents contain some very sensitive information. Borrowers are going to be sending over photo identification, bank statements, Social Security numbers (only if absolutely necessary), home addresses, and personal financial statements. You as a lender have an obligation to the borrower to maintain that information in a secure and private fashion.

Also, there are privacy considerations at play as well. You may be required to have a borrower sign a privacy policy that allows you the right to disclose specific private details to third-party vendors you work with in the normal business of closing a loan. If you have read the book this far, you know how many people might be involved in the process of a loan, and how those people will each require key information related the transaction, including the identity of the buyer, your prospective borrower.

You will also want a way to track what documentation has been provided and when that documentation was submitted. If there is a deadline looming for a closing but the borrower has not provided you with requested information until the morning of closing, you will likely not have enough time to adequately review the material. Having the ability to document what a borrower sent over and when can go a long way in establishing credibility as a lender when a borrower feels that you are dragging your feet to the detriment of their closing.

As for getting physical custody of documents in a digital age, we strongly recommend signing up for a subscription to a secure file-transfer service. For new lenders, this may be the most economical way to process documents, as having a lending platform can be cost prohibitive to lenders who only do a handful of transactions in a year. Secure file-transfer services will allow you to create folders and even certain file checklists that your borrower can then log into and upload to a secure site. These services also time-stamp the documents when they are uploaded to the portal, which allows you to see when documents were submitted.

Email is generally not a secure way to transfer sensitive information, and most free cloud-based storage systems are equally unsecure. Just think of who may have access to your accounts or passwords to your computer. You also want to protect the information from being obtained by someone in your physical location. If you print out documents with sensitive information, make sure they remain locked in areas where they cannot be accessed or read by unauthorized people. No matter the outcome of the lending opportunity, safe storage of those physical documents is still a requirement. It may even be best to destroy physical copies and keep secure copies of documents in digital form for ease of storage and space limitations.

RISKS AND REWARDS

By now you likely have a solid understanding of the risks involved in not thoroughly reviewing your borrower and the property and project. However, the reward you get in return for being extra cautious, detail-oriented, and almost sleuth-like is you will sleep well at night knowing your capital investment is as safe as it possibly could be.

If you feel you have received sufficient information to help you review the borrower's character, capacity, capital, collateral, and conditions, and you are still feeling good about the loan, this means your loan is "cleared to close," in traditional lender terminology. Congratulations on getting this far! The process of compiling all the documentation needed to underwrite your loan is a massive feat.

LESSONS LEARNED

Mike decided to do a loan for an investor who just purchased a large parcel of land at a steep discount from a tax foreclosure auction. Mike ordered a title commitment and it came back clean with no special exceptions to worry about, so he proceeded with a loan in the amount of $35,000 in first lien position. However, to save on costs and expedite the loan, Mike chose to create the loan documents himself using a template he'd found on the internet. He also decided not to involve an escrow closer, who would help order title insurance and record the necessary documents with the county.

Instead, Mike met the borrower at his local bank branch to sign the loan documents and have them notarized by a personal banker who was also a notary public. In exchange, he gave a cashier's check to the borrower and then left. Later that week, when Mike had more time available, he drove to the county clerk's office to record the deed of trust on the property.

A few months went by, and Mike's borrower stopped making payments. After several attempts to get the borrower to respond and pay his interest payments, Mike decided it was time to get an attorney involved to discuss next steps.

The attorney reviewed Mike's loan documents, and after ordering a new title commitment, found several key issues with the loan that would make legal recourse challenging.

First, the loan documents were written up inaccurately. More specifically, the deed of trust and promissory note were made to a legal business entity, but the signature lines were signed by the borrower as an individual and not as a member of the business entity. This could make the deed of trust possibly unenforceable.

Additionally, upon review of the new title commitment, the attorney noticed that Mike was not listed as the first lienholder but rather was in second position behind a rather large hard-money loan in the amount of $275,000. If that wasn't enough, the title had been transferred to a new business entity in between the time Mike's borrower signed the loan documents and Mike recorded them with the county. The new business entity was owned by the borrower's sister.

After the initial legal review, Mike's attorney contacted the legal counsel for the hard-money lender in first position. Since the hard-money lender had ordered proper title insurance with First American Title, they made a claim against their loan priority and the title company offered to pay out the loan and pursue legal action against Mike's borrower and his sister.

While this story ended up playing out fine for Mike, he learned a valuable lesson to utilize escrow closing services to transact all his future loans and to order a lender's title insurance policy with every loan as well. Mike would not be taking chances with do-it-yourself loans ever again.

COMPILE & CONDITION IN REVIEW

C

COMPILE & CONDITION
In this step, the goal is to receive and review all the necessary documents and information needed to underwrite and approve the loan for funding. This is a fact-finding mission where you put your private-detective cap on and sleuth through each document, looking for clues that will piece together a story about the borrower and the property being used as collateral.

P

PERSON
The primary person involved in this step is the borrower, as they are responsible for furnishing whatever documentation and evidence you may need to validate that what they told you is, in fact, realistic, accurate, reasonable, and truthful.

PROPERTY
For a fix-and-flip project, you will need to verify the property condition, project financials, and other aspects related to the rehab and resale of the property.

For a buy-and-hold investment, you will need to review the rental income potential, property condition, and refinancing requirements.

PAPERWORK
There is plenty of paperwork involved in this step! Here, you will need to verify documentation related to the borrower's character, capacity, capital, collateral, and conditions.

R

RISKS AND REWARDS
This can be the riskiest part of the loan process. Failure to do proper and thorough due diligence could lead to greater risks and challenges after the loan is funded. The rule of thumb is to find any and every reason you could possibly say no to this deal. This pessimistic approach can help you uncover potential issues that should be addressed before you fund OR reveal too many red flags, leading you to walk away from the deal.

CALL TO ACTION FOR COMPILE & CONDITION

1. Create a list of required documents you will be requesting from the borrower. This list should be customized to your own risk tolerance and comfort level.
2. Order a preliminary title commitment from a local title company for any properties you will be using to secure the loan as collateral.
3. Research vendors and service providers that will enable safe and secure transmission of borrower information and secure document retention or disposal.
4. Assess documents as they are submitted to establish if additional questions need to be addressed or additional documentation requested.
5. Establish a range for the value of the property.

Chapter 7

COMPOSE & CLOSE

CALCULATE & EVALUATE > CONNECT > CONTACT > COMPILE & CONDITION > **COMPOSE & CLOSE** > COLLECT & CONVEY

COMPOSE & CLOSE QUICK PEEK

C | **COMPOSE & CLOSE**
In this step, the goal is to have your legal loan documents created and take proper steps to fund the loan and receive signed documents in return.

P

PERSON
Here you shift from the main character to a supporting actor. Your attorney, closing agent, and borrower's insurance agent will be busy.

PROPERTY
The most important part of this step is to ensure proper protection on the property itself, with adequate levels and types of insurance.

PAPERWORK
You will be receiving signed loan documents from the closing, in addition to any last-minute due diligence items, such as insurance binders.

R | **RISKS AND REWARDS**
Even though you are more passively involved in this part of the loan process, you still need to catch errors others may have missed and check for continuity between documents.

Congratulations! You have made it through compiling borrower documents and reviewing them to get a better feel for your borrower and the property that will act as collateral for the loan. If you have decided to move forward with the loan, you are now in the next step of the loan cycle, Compose & Close. Here, you will have your attorney draw up the legal loan documentation required to close the loan. You may even have them review some of the supplemental documents, such as the borrower entity documents or the title commitment and any supplements, to make sure you are adequately covered.

Since you have done most of the heavy lifting up to this point, this step will be considerably more relaxed, as others will play key roles in helping to get your loan across the finish line. However, you still have plenty of work to do to make the idea of this loan opportunity into a real, legally binding contract between you and the borrower, so don't think it is time to set it and forget it. You will still need to be actively involved in moving the loan from attorney to escrow, keeping the borrower in the loop, and reviewing everyone's work to ensure it is accurate.

Think of this step as that famous line uttered at weddings: "Speak now or forever hold your peace." While no one is getting married, you are—in a way—marrying yourself to this loan for a mutually agreed-upon time frame. Therefore, this is the time to correct mistakes in the paperwork or alter any terms for the loan. Doing any of this after documents have been signed by the borrower and legally recorded becomes much more cumbersome and expensive—and that is if the borrower is even willing to alter things after the fact. We will go over specific things to look for in your legal loan documents and address conversations to have with various people in this step.

This step will be broken down into three tasks.

1. Requesting legal loan documents to be created by an attorney
2. Reviewing the loan documents prior to close and coordinating other parties
3. Facilitating the loan signing, recording, and funding

PERSON

A key person in this step is going to be you. Now, you may be thinking, "I've done all the analysis, I've read the documents, I'm comfortable! How much more is there to do?" The answer is "plenty." There are other people involved in this step, but it really boils down to you being the glue that holds it all together. As the lender, you have the responsibility to make sure the documents created on your behalf are accurate and legally sound. After all, it is your money being put on the line, so taking this level of ownership is important. Do not feel pressured or rushed, but do work expeditiously, as time is of the essence.

It is also crucial at this juncture to let your borrower know in writing of any final changes to the terms of the loan before moving forward with loan document preparation to ensure you are on the same page. This prevents any last minute surprises at the closing table, which can breed resentment into a new business relationship, or worse, make the borrower back out of the loan, leaving you with the attorney fees to pay.

Now is a good time to set clear expectations with the borrower, again preferably in writing, about what steps will happen next and by whom, and approximately how long each step will take. Many borrowers just assume the lender is responsible for all tasks up until the loan is funded. This could not be further from the truth. For example, if the closing agent is backed up with signing appointments and has not begun preparing your loan to close, the borrower could blame you for these problems. However, if you communicate to the borrower that their loan documents are completed and now with the escrow closer, they could reach out directly to escrow and request a status update rather than blame you for something out of your control.

Other Key Players

In short order, there are several other participants involved in the successful execution of this step. They include:

- **Attorney:** They will prepare the loan documents on your behalf and review any documents you may have concerns with, such as the title commitment, special exceptions, business-entity documents, etc.
- **Escrow closing agent:** This team is responsible for coordinating the signing, recording, and funding of your loan.
- **Borrower:** They will be required to sign the loan documents.
- **Notary public:** If documents are not signed at the escrow closing office, you will be assigned a mobile notary public, who will verify your identification and walk you through the signing of your loan package.
- **Loan servicer:** If you are going to contract out your loan servicing to a third party, this will be the time to engage their services.
- **Your banker:** This is someone with authorization at your local bank branch who can assist you with your wire transfer when ready.

Even though you might not be the main character in the Compose & Close step, since an attorney will draft up your loan documents and an escrow agent will help facilitate the actual closing of the loan, you are considered a key supporting character as well as the director.

Escrow Closer (Also Known as the Closing Agent)

The escrow closer, which could also be the title company, serves a central role in the closing process. In some states this could be an attorney who acts as the escrow closing agent, but more often it is a licensed escrow closer. Think of them as the conductor of an orchestra. They will be coordinating documents and funds between you, your attorney, the borrower, the seller, perhaps the seller's attorney, and the real estate transaction coordinator if they are also involved. As you can imagine, this is a lot of moving parts for the closing company, so even though you may not be as active of a participant as you were in the previous two steps, this is not the time to take your attention away. You are still responsible as the lender for having correct legal documents and reviewing the details of all closing documents.

Borrower

Aside from your attorney and the closing agent, the borrower is also going to be central to this process. Having done appropriate due diligence, you have verified that (a) the borrower has enough liquid assets to close on the loan, (b) the exit strategy is feasible, and (c) the borrower understands the loan terms. We have a detailed discussion of asset evaluation and what you might require of the borrower in Chapter Nine of this book. Hopefully you have been openly and actively communicating the terms of the loan with the borrower, so they shouldn't be surprised by the number they need to bring to the table on the day of closing. If there are some deficiencies with the hazard insurance, the borrower will also need to reach back out to their insurance agent to alter the coverage. Also in this step, make sure you know the identity of your borrower and that the borrower is consistently listed across all the documentation. If you have a business entity with multiple partners who are required to sign on debt with personal guaranties, make sure you know when and where each borrower will sign. In a post-COVID world, online digital closings are becoming more commonplace, and borrowers may not even be in the same area. If the closing agent does not do digital closings, it may involve overnighting documents to and from each borrower to sign appropriately. Keep this in mind, as this process can delay closing a couple of days at a minimum.

Your Banker

Another entity you may not have thought about in the process of doing a loan is your own bank. Most closing agents, whether it is an attorney or a licensed escrow closer, will require that funds be wired to their trust account, usually a minimum of twenty-four hours before closing but not until a signing appointment has been scheduled between the borrower and a notary public. (This could also be the closing agent, who is registered as a notary public, signing the borrower in their office or dispatching a mobile notary to come out to the borrower and sign them at a location more convenient). You, as the lender, will need to communicate with your bank to find out the process and timeline for doing a wire transfer. Some larger banks, like Bank of America, have busy branches and require an appointment for a wire transfer. Just be sure to add in the necessary time to schedule an appointment and complete your wire transfer before the wire cutoff time. Some banks require several layers of management approvals, depending on the amount being transferred. This can add even more time to the process if the manager is at a different branch. You will want to be sure your wire transfer can be initiated before you leave the branch. Ask your banker to provide you with a follow-up email or call to let you know when it's been sent.

We discuss the process of wiring funds to closing agents in more detail in the Paperwork section, but realize there is a very narrow window between the time documents are ready to be signed and the time the loan will be ready to fund; and closing agents can set their own rules and timelines that you will need to adhere to.

PROPERTY

Most of your due diligence on the property has been completed by now. At this point, you only need to confirm the property condition is not any worse off than when you first visited. Depending on the length of time between the initial inspection of the property and closing day, you may want to have a quick update on the condition of the property. This can be done with a live videoconference call with the borrower, or a quick drive-by if you live in proximity to the property. You may also choose to skip this step since the property will undergo some significant renovations and the condition may not be relevant. However, you will at least want to confirm that there are no squatters on the property, which would require attention prior to close. Some closings take longer than originally planned due to title issues, so don't just assume the property is in the same shape it was during the initial inspection or submission of documents.

Other things to double-check are the closing date and the starting date listed on the hazard insurance and any other insurance that covers the physical structure of the property, such as hurricane, flood, or earthquake. You do not want the hazard insurance policy to start a day or more after closing. If the property burned down the night after closing and the policy didn't go into effect until the next day, that incident is likely not covered. The borrower would then be responsible for bearing the entire financial burden of rebuilding or repairing, and you would face a loss of principal because of the deterioration in value.

The hazard insurance policy and declaration page should also be available to you before closing, and a policy quote should be provided to the closing agent if the borrower wishes to have the insurance policy paid for at closing. You are reviewing this document for appropriate coverage limits and to ensure that you are added as a mortgagee or loss payee on the declaration page of the policy. This protects you as the lender should a claim be made on the policy, and notifies you if the policy is cancelled or allowed to lapse due to nonpayment. Also, in the event of a total-loss claim, you will be paid from the claim for any covered events to the property.

PAPERWORK

The first task you will need to complete in the Compose & Close step is to request that legal documents be drafted on your behalf based on your mutually agreed-upon terms with the borrower. Once drafted, you will need to review the legal documents for accuracy, coordinate tasks between the borrower and closing agent, and project-manage the loan up until it is funded. Remember, all you get in return for the money you have wired to the closing agent are your legally binding, signed, and notarized documents! These documents help keep your capital safe and give you rights to recover any losses sustained. You want to make sure you are comfortable with the terms and coverages and that the borrower understands them. This will all result in a streamlined closing.

Legal Documents Provided by an Attorney

Listed below is a quick summary of the paperwork we suggest you review before sending any money to the closing.

Promissory Note

Probably one of the most critical documents in the packet, the promissory note outlines the legal terms of the loan, including duration, payment and interest specifications, and what happens in the event of default.

Lien Instrument (Mortgage or Deed of Trust)

This document is prepared for and filed with the local municipality (generally the county or township) in which the borrower's property that is being used as collateral for the loan resides. This document essentially places a lien on the property. In other words, the property cannot be sold without permission from the lender or until the debt is relieved. Once the loan is fully reimbursed, the lien will be removed on the property via a reconveyance filed with the county.

Assignment of Rents

This document states that if the borrower falls behind or defaults on the loan, the rents will be assigned to the lender. Even if the property is intended for a fix-and-flip, it is good to have this clause created in case the borrower decides to turn the property into a rental.

Closing Instructions

The closing instructions outline how the loan funds will be handled, as well as the other procedural aspects of the closing process as stipulated by the preparer of the loan documents, which is the attorney. The closing instructions will direct the closing agent on what steps to take on behalf of the lender, including how funds are to be disbursed; order the Lender's Title Policy in a specified amount; and, in some cases, require a review period of the signed and notarized documents before authorizing the closing agent to release to record. Generally, the attorney who prepares the other legal documents on behalf of the lender will create closing instructions when requested.

There may be other legal instruments your attorney advises you to create or provide, such as loan disclosures. These are state-specific so be sure to find out from your attorney in advance so you can familiarize yourself with what additional legal documents you may need and why they are important.

Most people think the promissory note is the most important document in the closing process if you are the lender. While it is important, an even more important document is the lien instrument: the mortgage or deed of trust. This document is recorded with the local municipal clerk of courts and becomes public record. Without this document being executed (signed) and then recorded at the local municipal courthouse, there is no record *anywhere* of you having a lien on that property. Without that lien recorded, you essentially have an unsecured loan, which is not something you want!

Once all the legal instruments are prepared by your attorney, you will want to check both the promissory note and the lien instrument to make sure the pertinent details are correct and align. Both documents should be reviewed very carefully to ensure dates, names, addresses, parcel numbers, legal descriptions, and dollar amounts are all accurate, according to your loan rates and terms provided to your attorney. The promissory note will contain different information from a lien instrument, but names, addresses, and amounts should still correspond on each when presented on both documents. Loan terms such as length, interest rates, and other factors like prepayment penalties and other fees being rolled into the loan are itemized out in the promissory note but not in the lien instrument. The mortgage or deed of trust, on the other hand, has a lot of language centered around the laws of default and foreclosure, how the title can be conveyed, if at all, without triggering a due-on-sale clause, and any additional clauses such as "no junior liens are allowed after the first mortgage."

Once you have reviewed these documents and your attorney has completed the final draft ready for escrow, you will share these documents directly with the escrow closer, unless your attorney will do so on your behalf. Either way is fine as long as the closing agent has your attorney's contact information should they need clarification on any of the documents.

When sending over the final, unsigned loan package to escrow, you will also want to send the closing agent the loan servicing documents required to set up the account and begin servicing the loan after close. This will be the onboarding paperwork required by the servicing company to set up the account with the specific parameters of the loan. The servicer must have all the pertinent loan rates and terms in order to maintain the account for the duration of the loan. It is also important that the servicer receives authorization and account information to allow for an automatic ACH withdrawal of funds each month from the borrower's specified bank account and a deposit directly into a bank account of your choice. The servicer may be able to break out payments from multiple accounts as well, which is handy for lenders who wish to fund deals as a partnership.

With your legal documents and loan servicing setup documents in hand, the closing agent will start preparing your loan file for signing by the borrower. One of the most crucial documents the closer will prepare is a HUD-1 Closing Statement, also known as a settlement statement. This document is prepared on behalf of the borrower (and seller, in the case of a purchase), and breaks down all costs associated with closing a loan both for the borrower and for the lender. It outlines what fees are payable to you, if any, as the lender, what costs are charged for title, escrow, and loan servicing setup, and how much money the borrower needs to tender at close, if any, and how much you, as the lender, are required to tender at close. If you disagree with any of the amounts on the HUD-1, this is the time to have them corrected.

It is important you review the draft settlement statement as soon as it has been prepared by the closing agent. It is not uncommon to see errors and omissions on the draft settlement statement, especially in recent years with the onslaught of real estate purchases and refinance transactions as a result of lower interest rates and white-hot real estate markets. In our market, we had closing agents we do business with regularly share with us that their transaction volumes had tripled while they were also short-staffed. Therefore, make sure you review this closely to ensure everything looks accurate. If you are concerned you will miss something, you may wish to ask the real estate agent who drafted your loan documents to review it for you as well.

The final piece of documentation the escrow closing agent will prepare and send to you is the wire instructions. These are written instructions from the escrow closing agent that specify how much to wire and provide account information for the company's escrow trust account. It is imperative to receive these instructions directly from the escrow company and to follow up and verify the account information directly with a representative at the escrow company.

Ideally, you want the time between signing and notarizing, recording, and distribution of funds to be as minimal as possible. In the best scenario, you will not authorize the escrow closer to release funds to the borrower until recording numbers come back from the appropriate municipality (typically a county or township, depending on where you live), but some areas do not have the ability to record the mortgage or deed of trust within a twenty-four to forty-eight hour time frame. If your area takes significantly longer to record, you may need to release funds before recording numbers come back. There is always a remote possibility that some other lien or encumbrance could be placed against the property during the window in which your loan documents are being recorded; however, certain title insurance policies and clauses can safeguard you from these types of scenarios in what is commonly referred to as the "gap period."

RISKS AND REWARDS

Speaking of wire instructions, a word of warning here: This part is a total gut punch! One of the most pivotal aspects of this step is going to be actually funding the loan, and this part comes with some significant risk in the form of wire fraud. We are bringing this up here because you will be required to wire funds from your bank account directly to escrow. For those of you who have never had to wire money, be prepared, as this process can be a bit jarring the first few times you do it. It is a lot of money to ship out of your account all at once! And with the increase in cybersecurity breaches, malicious activity around hacking into company email accounts and transmitting fake wire instructions is on the rise. There is no need to panic, as you can easily avoid becoming a victim of wire fraud by following some simple instructions.

The Wire Transfer Process

Each bank will have its own process, so ask early on about the requirements to wire funds from your account to another account. Some banks will allow you to do it online, while others need you to come in and sign a form or process the request over the phone. Knowing the process and timeline is important. If you are new to making wire transfers, we suggest going into your bank branch and having a banker assist you so you do not make mistakes.

The first step is to receive wire instructions from your escrow closer. These will either be sent by secured email or fax. Although faxes are still widely considered the safest form of electronic communication transmittal, most lenders do not have access to a fax machine or line. Once these instructions are sent to you, call the escrow office and validate the information provided. This information should include the total amount of the wire transfer required to fund the loan, a reference for the transfer, which typically includes the escrow file number and/or the property address, and the banking information for the escrow company's trust account, including account number, routing number, and physical branch address.

As mentioned earlier, wire fraud is a rampant problem. Documents can be altered online to look so similar to the originals that it is nearly impossible to notice the difference. We are going to quickly outline the steps for verifying wiring instructions here because this is one place that you could potentially lose all your capital if you were given fraudulent information.

Verify wire instructions with the escrow closing company by calling into the office. For security purposes, we advocate you independently look up the phone number for the closing agent. Do not use a phone number provided by anyone from an email or embedded within the wire instructions provided. If intercepted by scammers, your wire instructions could have a false phone number listed, not just the bank account. Look up the number yourself, call the number, and make sure it is the correct office. Even better, call your actual closing team and speak directly to them since they are familiar with your loan transaction.

Ask the closing agent to verify the wiring instructions. Have the closing agent read the information to you. Do *not* read numbers to them and have them agree to it. Compare what you're told over the phone to the instructions you received.

Now that you have verified the wiring instructions from a number you independently found for the closing company, it is time to work with your bank or whatever your source of funds is for this loan. We are going to describe the process as if you called the bank yourself to initiate a wire, as that is currently the most common way to request a wire.

Call the number for your bank that, again, you have independently verified. Do not use a phone number on any email correspondence, especially if it comes from anyone involved in the transaction. You can usually find a contact number when you log into your online account with your bank. This would be the safest way to get a verified phone number. When you are routed to the right department or person, the process will begin.

The bank representative will likely ask you a series of questions before beginning. The questions focus on how you received the wiring instructions, if there were any last-minute changes to the wiring instructions made, if you know the entity or person receiving the wired money, what the purpose of the wire is, and how much money the wire will be for. While these questions can be grueling, you will feel more secure in the process knowing you located the information yourself, verified it yourself, and you are ready to fund.

Once the grilling is done, you will need to provide the routing number and bank account number for the wire. You will likely need the name of the bank that the funds are going to and possibly even the address of that bank. You will also need the name of the account holder. Most closing attorneys have an account that is used specifically for wiring, and they frequently have titles for the account such as Closing Agent Name–Trust Account or Escrow Account. All of this information should be on the wiring instructions sheet, if you were supplied with one before your call, to verify it from the closing agent. The process should be as simple as reading the information to the bank representative. After you have shared that information with the bank representative, they will likely repeat everything back to you for verification and accuracy.

This whole process may take about ten minutes. We strongly advocate you do this in a quiet place when you are not in a rush. These are important details, from the amount of money being wired to the account details and so much more. Take the time to do it without distractions. This might be the largest sum of money you have sent to anyone else at any one time in your life. Make sure it is correct, that you feel confident in the information provided to you, and that you have relayed it correctly.

The risks here center largely around inconsistencies and inaccuracies in the paperwork involved in the closing process. Some larger risks in this process will be discussed in sections below so you can be prepared to address them. The rewards are that you will have successfully funded your first loan and potentially made your first income from a private loan through origination points and other fees you may charge the borrower.

Be sure to ask about cutoff times for same-day wire requests, as most banks have a specific time after which they cannot guarantee the wire will go through that same day.

Recording Timelines

We mentioned earlier about verifying the process and timeline the closing agent uses to record the necessary documents related to the closing. If your lien isn't recorded, the borrower could obtain another mortgage on the property. The new company would not be aware of any existing liens, which would allow them to do the closing and get their lien recorded ahead of yours. Now you may be in a second lien position, and when the two loans are combined, you might be left with a borrower owing more on the property than it is worth. This is a very uncomfortable place to be as a lender. Discuss with the closing company how quickly the lien instruments are filed for recording after a closing and when you can expect to receive the originals. Some companies will overnight documents to the clerk of court to be recorded the next day. Others may messenger them in bundles, and still others may stick them in the regular postal mail to be recorded whenever the mail gets delivered and the clerks get around to recording the documents. There may be title policy riders that can be added to cover potential problems like this, which is why it is good to understand what is being included in the lender's title insurance that you are requiring the borrower to purchase. There is also an option for title insurance called "gap coverage" that insures the title for those days between closing and recording to guarantee your lien position on the property. This may be helpful if there is a lien already out on the property but it hasn't been recorded yet and is discovered after closing and recording.

In this step, there is certainly a lot more risk than reward. You have put in a lot of hard work up to this point, but this is the one hurdle between you and earning some passive income. The risks here are considerably larger than in previous steps because this is when it becomes legally binding between multiple parties. Think of how many vendors are involved in this process: attorney, closing agent, title insurance, hazard insurance, any real estate agents involved in the transaction, the seller, and then you. The person bringing the most amount of money to this closing is going to be you as the lender. It is on you to make sure you are protected as well as the asset that is acting as collateral.

Skimp Now, Pay Later

There is a lot of temptation for beginning private lenders to use canned loan documents they find online such as through LegalZoom or Nolo. The issue with this route is that you cannot be sure your documents are thorough enough to protect you and are compliant with your state-specific private lending regulations and usury laws. The other disadvantage is you do not have the access you may need to a local real estate attorney should you have questions about how to proceed. This can be an invaluable resource when first starting out.

Some of you may think you are doing better than online legal documents by having a local real estate attorney draft up a boilerplate template you can use over and over again instead of paying an attorney to draft up loan documents with each deal you fund. While a step above finding generic templates online, boilerplate templates can become an issue if you do not fill them in properly. For example, if you have templates drawn up by your attorney that are for an individual or possibly a couple to sign, but you now have a loan opportunity with a business entity or a trust, the signature lines will not appear in the proper format. If contested in court, your documents could come under scrutiny if the borrower did not sign in the manner legally required.

To play it safe, until you get the hang of things, ask your local real estate attorney to draft loan documents for each deal. If you are only lending out on one loan at a time and a long period of time transpires between each of your deals, you may want to use an attorney for a while since you will need to refresh yourself with the basics until it becomes second nature. If you are concerned about costs, you can pass through these costs to your borrower. We do this as part of our lender fees and rarely does someone balk at it.

If you cannot find a local real estate attorney you love working with, there is another option. As we have mentioned a few times already, Geraci LLP is a national law firm specializing in private lending law and advocacy, and serves as the general counsel for the American Association of Private Lenders (AAPL). Based in Irvine, California, this well-known firm within the private lending industry provides a wide array of services to private lenders, both big and small. For smaller private lenders, one of the greatest services they offer is canned loan document templates tailored to state-specific needs. This service is called

Lightning Docs and it requires you to input the critical loan information, so you will need to pay special attention to the accuracy of your data entry. Their team of attorneys is always available to help answer any questions you may have about a loan or specific clause in the loan documents as well. There are some setup charges, annual maintenance fees, and a per-use charge for each set of loan documents, but these documents will do a far better job of protecting your interests (and your principal investment) than anything else available online. Check out the resources at www.biggerpockets.com/lendingbonus for more information about the team and services offered by the Geraci LLP Firm.

LESSONS LEARNED

Jamie, a small private lender, was speaking to Malcolm about a loan that he needed to rehab his late mother's home. He wanted it in perfect condition before placing it on the market. The property was now owned by Malcolm and his sister, Charla, a working mom who was too busy to handle the details of the rehab or loan but was on board with the plans to renovate so they could achieve maximum market value. Or so it seemed. Since Malcolm assured Jamie that his busy sister, Charla, would have no issues with the loan and was fully aware of the project he was initiating, she moved forward with having loan documents drafted and was careful to make sure both brother and sister were named on the loan documents. When the mobile notary finally reached out to schedule a signing appointment, Charla was not prepared for or compliant with the loan being taken out. It turns out that Malcolm had never told Charla about needing a loan for the rehab. She was distraught by the fact that this was coming out of left field and refused to sign loan documents. Jamie was surprised by the turn of events and learned her lesson to always contact with every material participant in the loan as early as possible. In this case, Jamie was left without an interest-bearing loan and had to pay legal fees for the loan documents that were drafted up on her behalf.

COMPOSE & CLOSE IN REVIEW

C

COMPOSE & CLOSE

In this step, the goal is to have your legal loan documents created in order to move forward with closing and funding the loan using a third-party escrow closer. Most of your due diligence work should have been taken care of in the previous step. Now you will be in more of a review-and-approve role while others work to get the loan across the finish line. But don't take your eye off the ball; you may be needed for an assist!

P

PERSON	PROPERTY	PAPERWORK
Here you shift from the main character to a supporting actor while others step in to help you out. Other players in this phase include some form of legal resource to help prepare the necessary documents, the borrower to sign the loan docs, an escrow closer (typically a third-party escrow company or an attorney, depending on your state requirements and your personal preference), and a representative from your bank.	The most important part of this step is to ensure proper protection on the property itself. This includes an appropriate hazard insurance policy and any extra coverage that may be necessary for the area or property, such as flood or earthquake insurance as well as a lender's title insurance policy.	The paperwork here is pretty straightforward and includes the loan docs, the insurance policies, and any closing documents. Fortunately you have others working diligently on your behalf to prepare the loan to close and fund.

R

RISKS AND REWARDS

Even though you are more passively involved in this part of the loan process, you still need to pay attention to the details when reviewing the loan documents and other paperwork provided to you. Not catching errors could lead to legal problems later down the line. And if you aren't herding the involved parties, you could run the risk of not being able to close on time.

CALL TO ACTION FOR COMPOSE & CLOSE

1. Independently verify all information for the closing agent and wiring instructions.
2. Learn your bank's wiring process and timeline.
3. Read through all documents for accuracy in loan terms, property address, purchase price, proper borrower names, and how the title will be held.
4. Assess the closing statement, HUD-1, for accuracy of fees associated with your loan, including recording fees.
5. Verify that adequate insurances are in place and appropriate for type of property, renovation level, and exit strategy.
6. Conduct post-closing assessment for receipt of documents that are due to the lender.

Chapter 8

COLLECT & CONVEY

| CALCULATE & EVALUATE | CONNECT | CONTACT | COMPILE & CONDITION | COMPOSE & CLOSE | **COLLECT & CONVEY** |

COLLECT & CONVEY QUICK PEEK

C	**COLLECT & CONVEY**
	You are almost across the finish line! The most rewarding part of the loan process is finally being able to sit back and collect interest payments. You will also have to prepare some items when it comes time to have the loan fully repaid.

P	**PERSON**	**PROPERTY**	**PAPERWORK**
	This is when you and the borrower take over, unless a loan servicer will be involved in collecting your monthly payments and providing end-of-year tax statements.	This is the time when you may choose to conduct site visits and ensure contractors and subs are being handled properly.	The paperwork here is monthly statements from a loan servicer if being use, and receipts of payments received.

R	**RISKS AND REWARDS**
	The temptation in this phase may be to sit back and watch the money roll in to your bank account, but failure to stay involved in the project progress or, at minimum, to ensure your loan payments are current could lead to big problems.

Congratulations on closing your loan! You finally made it. The loan documents were drawn up, signed, legally recorded, and funded. This was a lot of effort to ensure your loan was safely placed in the right hands. Now the easy part—sitting back and collecting what we like to call "mailbox money." Even if you wish to defer monthly installment payments until the loan is repaid in full, you will still earn interest income that will help you realize some of your investing goals. Whether you choose to receive monthly payments or not, you will still need to have some regular communication with your borrower throughout the duration of you loan. It will be important to identify if a project is getting off track and progress is slowing down.

This step has two distinct parts.

1. Collecting payments and receiving status updates until the loan is ready to be repaid
2. Preparing for the loan repayment and conveying the loan once it has been paid off

We will also share with you how to protect your capital investment after the loan has funded by outlining techniques to help you identify project challenges and delays before they escalate out of control. Should the borrower not be performing, these techniques can allow you to regain control of the collateral or help the investor finish the project without going into the foreclosure process.

Staying Connected after Close

As you have seen in the previous steps, the tremendous amount of flexibility you have within private lending can be both a blessing and a curse. While this flexibility may make it harder to figure out the "rules of the road," it also allows you to tailor your budding business to your own preferences. You can choose to work in certain markets, with certain property types, and maybe even with certain types of borrowers, whether it's active investors or borrowers with full-time W-2 jobs. This last step, Collect & Convey, is no different from any previous one when it comes to flexibility. Remember way back in the pre-step, Calculate & Evaluate, when we asked why you were investing in real estate through private lending? That guidance will be particularly helpful in this step.

The flexibility here centers largely around how active you want to be while the money is deployed as a loan with the borrower. Some lenders don't want to be kept appraised of major updates on the property, while others want to do weekly video calls. That's just one example of how different lenders can be during the loan. Again, know what your communication expectations about the project are so you can accurately convey that to a borrower.

Some things all lenders should be aware of, regardless of how often they receive updates, include:

- Are all monthly installment payments current?
- Is the project progressing smoothly or is it in jeopardy of schedule delays, which could affect repayment?
- Is the project on budget and are there any labor or service disputes you should be aware of?
- Have there been any material changes to the initial exit strategy? If so, what are they?

While we did discuss some of the levers you can pull to tweak loan terms to offer more safety for you as a lender and possibly create more of a win-win scenario with your borrower, one we didn't mention was the payment portion of the loan terms. There are many different ways to handle the fees, interest, and origination points that you may charge a borrower. We will give you an idea of the options and some pros and cons to each, but ultimately it will be up to you, your risk tolerances, and your life choices to decide how to receive those payments. No two lenders will do it the same way, and the same lender may not do the same payment structure for every single loan. Think of it like this: We will tell you what food is on the buffet line, but we won't tell you what to eat. If you ever have questions about payment, reach out to a real estate attorney or other private lenders, but also consider what you may need as a borrower both in terms of income and assurance so you can sleep easy at night.

If you are lending as an individual, one thing we advocate for is setting up a separate account for receiving payment deposits that is not your main family bank account. If you opt to receive payments electronically without using a servicing company, you may disclose bank account and routing numbers to a borrower for payments. While that allows them to put money into the account, it can also potentially allow them to take it out too! Once the payment has been deposited, you can transfer it to any account you so choose.

If you are lending as a business entity, you can also use this arrangement but keep it within your business entity. Do not have a borrower send payments to a personal account. In addition, having a separate account for payments will help you keep track of exactly what has been paid and by whom if you have multiple loans out at once. You won't have to go searching through your online shopping purchases to find the few borrower payments when it comes tax time. Again, this is merely a suggestion, but how you have this set up can be equally flexible, depending on your needs and the laws centered around business entity versus personal income.

PERSON

The people involved in the Collect & Convey step will be (a) your borrower, who will be making payments (should you choose to have them make payments during the term of the loan), (b) a loan servicing company, which will be handling the payment should you choose to not use a loan servicer, (c) a potential inspector or general contractor who will verify work has been done and paid for, and (d) you, the lender.

Borrower Communication

You will need to decide how often you want to receive updates on a project. This is a personal choice. Establish what will make you comfortable and how involved you want to be. For some lenders, being actively involved in regular updates on a project feels akin to babysitting the borrower. Instead, these types of lenders prefer a more passive approach and may reduce their LTV guidelines to add equity as protection in case something goes wrong during the loan. If you choose to receive updates, you will want to ask about current progress, potential challenges, and any impacts to the budget or timeline.

Loan Servicing Provider Updates

You likely will not need to connect with loan servicer unless you need a status update on a payment. Good servicers will handle the borrower notice of late payment without letting you know and will proactively reach out to you if there is an update on the status of your loan. One note of a caution, however: There is a lot of disenchantment with contract loan service companies nationwide. Poor customer service, inaccurate or missed payment processing, and calculation errors on payoff demands are known to happen. Until you have a solid working relationship with a preferred vendor you trust, you may choose to actively monitor your loan to ensure it's being serviced properly.

PROPERTY

Property considerations during this step will be largely focused on the renovation process, progress toward exit strategy, and if the insurance stays current or changes after renovations are complete and the property becomes an active rental. Some lenders feel it is important to have regular check-ins with the general contractor overseeing the project or pay an independent inspector to tour the project. However, when starting out in private lending on basic cosmetic fix-and-flip projects, the latter is an unnecessary expense typically used for large, complex renovation projects with big budgets and rehab money held back.

Aside from requesting regular project status updates, some of the techniques you can use to identify current or potential challenges that may affect budget or create delays include:

- Requesting proof of permits as they are received.
- Requesting copies of permit inspection sign-offs as they are received.
- Requiring lien release waivers to be signed by every laborer who works on the jobsite. This will help to ensure all laborers and subcontractors are satisfied and have been paid. They are required to be furnished at the time of sale.
- Ordering an updated title supplement on your loan to identify any new encumbrances, liens, or judgments that may have appeared after the loan was funded.
- If local, driving by the property to see how progress may be going.

One other concern about the property during this step occurs if the loan goes into default. The most obvious reason for defaulting on a loan is financial nonperformance. However, there are other reasons that could cause the loan to go into default. Be sure to have a conversation with your real estate attorney who drafted up your loan documents about what legally constitutes a default on your loan and what does not.

Example of potential nonfinancial default considerations include:

- If the borrower lets the property insurance lapse and does not remedy it immediately.
- If the borrower moves into the property at any time during the loan term.
- If the borrower does not perform against timelines or key milestones identified in the loan.
- If the borrower destroys any buildings on the property.
- If the property taxes are significantly past due.
- If the property has additional charges, liens, or encumbrances.

These are just a few of the possible ways to default on a loan, even if the monthly installment payment is current. Your attorney can advise you on what standard clauses are allowable for the state in which the property is located. We suggest you have them walk you through the actual language on the mortgage or deed of trust so you can see what legally is presented and how that affects your loan.

PAPERWORK

Once the property is stabilized (fully renovated and ready for sale, or renovated and rented), your loan moves into the Convey part of this step. Here, you will be repaid in full by the borrower through either a sale of the property or refinance of the loan. There are some actions you will do for that process to be complete.

Payoff Statement (Payoff Demand)

The first step is to have a final payoff demand generated. This is an official document prepared by the loan servicer stating how much interest is still owed, how much the principal loan amount is, and what other fees are going to be charged to the borrower for reconveying the loan off the property and closing out the account. Payoff statements are very important, so it is especially important that they be done correctly. The amount of the payoff needs to be accurate and in accordance with the promissory note down to a penny. In most cases it may not become an issue, but if there is ever any disagreement about the loan and it was discovered you overcharged the borrower on the payoff, it could be a problem. Again, this is something your loan servicing company will do for you, which is another reason you may want to consider having a third-party servicer for your loan.

Removing the Loan Off the Property's Title

If you are in a mortgage state, your real estate attorney can draw up a satisfaction of mortgage for you. Some closing agents may also be able to draw up a satisfaction of mortgage as part of their closing costs associated with a refinance or the sale of the property. If you live in a deed state, like we both do, you will need your trustee to look over the loan to prepare a full reconveyance to remove the deed of trust off the property.

End-of-Year Statements

As mentioned earlier, interest income will need to be reported as taxable income. This is handled through the creation of Form 1099-INT for lenders on interest income earned and Form 1098-INT for borrowers on interest income paid. Using a third-party servicing company that generates these forms on your behalf makes closing out your loan that much easier!

RISKS AND REWARDS

Risks in this step revolve around nonperformance of the loan, delays in renovations or ability to refinance out, and late-payment occurrences. It could be as small as your borrower forgetting what day it is and missing the payment deadline by a few days, or it could be as serious as your borrower being unreachable and no one working on the project.

Choosing Corrective Action

If the loan is in default in any way, you will need to know what your options are for curing the default or getting the project back on course. Depending on the situation, you may choose a more relaxed approach, or you may choose to proceed with legal action right away. In order to understand the best options available to you, you should consult with a local real estate attorney who specializes in foreclosure cases, and possibly bankruptcy proceedings as well. While we will outline the basic types of corrective action you could consider, your most sound advice will come from the legal counsel you talk to about your specific circumstances.

Force Placed Insurance

If your borrower's hazard insurance has lapsed, you will likely be notified as the mortgagee. (This is why being the lender listed on the insurance binder is so important!) There are a couple options available to you in order to ensure your loan remains protected in the event the property is physically damaged. The easiest solution would be to pay the insurance premiums yourself and add that expense to the final loan payoff demand at the end of the loan. In some circumstances, however, the carrier may cancel the policy and not allow the lender to reinstate it. This means you will have to obtain a different insurance policy from another carrier. This is called "force placed insurance" and can be cumbersome to obtain. However, it's imperative to find proper hazard insurance coverage so that your capital investment is protected.

Loan Extension

If your borrower is delayed by a few weeks or a month or two, you may choose to simply extend the current loan terms. This is the best option if the project is close to being put on the market or already listed and waiting to go under contract. The sale is eminent at this point, so the property will likely be sold before you can complete the foreclosure process. If your borrower is someone you would like to work with again in the future, this is a more relaxed and mutually beneficial approach to solving the default loan status. Plus, the borrower will appreciate your leniency and the ease of doing business with you.

Loan Modification

If your borrower needs additional funds in order to complete the project and you deem it to be both necessary and reasonably safe given the increase in value of the property to date, then you may want to consider doing a loan modification of the loan amount and possibly other terms. For example, if the project is behind schedule because of city inspection delays or supplier cost increases, you may want to add on the additional funds necessary to cover carrying costs or the additional cost of materials. Price adjustments on commodities such as lumber, windows, and concrete happen fairly frequently, and it is not uncommon for prices to change drastically from the time the project was bid out to the time materials were finally ordered for the job. Use your best judgment if a loan modification is warranted and would help protect your capital investment rather than force you to file foreclosure.

Deed in Lieu of Foreclosure

If the borrower chooses to walk away from a project, which has been known to happen, you can always try to negotiate a deed in lieu of foreclosure. This means the borrower will deed over their vested ownership to you in order to avoid legal foreclosure proceedings. This will save time and legal expenses, but be sure to check with your local real estate attorney on whether this is permitted in your state.

Understanding Foreclosure

This is legal action taken in court to repossess the property and put it up for sale at public auction, with proceeds going to repay the principal loan amount and any interest owed—including default interest, late fees, and any legal costs you assume. There are two types of foreclosures, depending on the state the property resides in.

- **Judicial foreclosures:** Where the foreclosing party files a lawsuit against the borrower and the case goes through the court system
- **Nonjudicial foreclosures:** Where the foreclosing party follows state-specific procedures outside of the court system

Generally speaking, non-judicial foreclosure states are less time-consuming and can therefore be less expensive as well. You will need to find an attorney who practices foreclosure law in order to understand your legal rights and the legal process required to recover what is owed to you.

Deficiency Judgment

What happens if the property is foreclosed and sold at public auction for less than your loan amount, unpaid interest, late fees, and legal costs? In this case, you can go after the borrowers who personally guaranteed the loans in a legal proceeding called a "deficiency judgment." This is where you will seek to collect directly from the borrower(s) on any remaining debt you were shorted after the property was sold at auction. This also a state-specific topic of conversation you will need to have with your foreclosure attorney. They will advise you on all legal recourse available to you, the differences between your options, and the potential consequences of each action.

The bottom line when addressing loans in default is to understand the path of least resistance in getting your loan repaid in full so you can move on to the next deal and start fresh again. While jumping to legal action might seem the safest bet for some more conservative and anxious lenders, you could find this process very time-consuming. You will also incur out-of-pocket legal costs, as you will be responsible for paying all legal fees in advance, even though you could recover these costs during the final repayment of the loan through auction. Explore which option will save you from the most headaches, create the best possible win-win scenario, and allows your loan to be paid off faster than you could through foreclosure.

LESSONS LEARNED

Carson was working his way through his third private loan when the borrower started avoiding his phone calls and not returning his texts. This was the first loan he had done with this borrower, who came recommended by some other investors in his local real estate market as someone experienced at doing fix-and-flips. Carson looked into the history of the properties this borrower had bought and sold over the past couple of years and even spoke with a few business references who consistently conveyed similar messages that the borrower was a hard worker and always held up his word. Knowing this, it troubled Carson when suddenly the communication dropped off when he was looking to get updates on progress of the borrower's latest project that Carson had funded.

The monthly loan payment went from a few days to a few weeks late, with no response from the borrower. Carson drove by the property to see what work had been done and saw that it sat empty with a half-filled construction dumpster in the driveway. Carson felt a knot in his stomach grow. Had the borrower taken on more than he could chew? Was the investor focusing on other houses and falling behind on this project and running low on money? Every imaginable terrible possibility ran through Carson's mind. He had agreed to lend out $150,000 on this property. While it had a healthy amount of equity, Carson did not want to manage a construction project of this magnitude and didn't know how to start foreclosure proceedings if it was warranted.

Carson decided to review his loan file and notes back at home to see if he could find any other contact information. He found the name and number of the investor who referred the borrower to him originally and decided to call. Carson explained the situation and asked if he knew what may be going on with his friend. The investor said that Carson's borrower had been in and out of the hospital with severe heart problems for the past month and was currently in the hospital recovering from open-heart surgery. While it made Carson feel better that his borrower was not intentionally dodging his calls or stretched thin on multiple projects, it did make him worry about how the loan was going to proceed, seeing that his borrower's health was severely impacting his ability to perform on the property and the loan as agreed.

Carson felt there were a few options he could try given this new information. If he chose forbearance, giving Carson a few months to recover and get back on track, then he may be able to collect that interest missed as one lump sum in a few months when the home sold. Working out the timing in his head, he figured that payment would show up in time for his oldest child's college tuition bill, so that option sounded appealing. Plus, he wouldn't have to go through foreclosure, which scared him. It could take awhile, and he really didn't want to take on a property that was halfway through a major renovation. Carson also felt that forbearance may just be delaying the inevitable. There were no assurances that his borrower would get better to the point that he could continue to manage a real estate business, much less a profitable one.

After consulting with his attorney, Carson decided to pursue a deed in lieu of foreclosure with the borrower. Thankfully, after a few weeks the borrower was home recovering and very apologetic about the delay in payment and communication. The attorney had walked Carson through the various options, and he felt getting custody of the property to get his money back out by way of a sale was the best path forward for everyone. After speaking with the borrower and explaining his position, the borrower agreed to sign over the property to Carson, as he didn't know how his health would be in the near future. The borrower was appreciative that Carson hadn't pursued more aggressive means such as filing a notice of default or starting legal proceedings, because he still wanted to pursue real estate should his health allow him to in the future. It would have made borrowing money a lot harder to have a foreclosure show up under his name!

In this case, Carson had done plenty of due diligence and everything "checked out" with the borrower. He had the experience, recommendations of many in the community, and the capital to complete the project. In Carson's mind this would be an easy transaction. What he didn't take into consideration was life itself happening to his borrower.

Carson ended up selling the property to the investor who recommended the borrower to him in the first place and was able to get his original capital back, plus the interest he was owed. Having a low loan-to-value, combined with a borrower who faced problems head-on, allowed Carson to come through the process financially unscathed. He felt that he never would have known his borrower was in the hospital if the borrower hadn't missed a payment, and it reminded Carson to look into the project a bit more. Had Carson decided to allow interest charges to be paid at the end of the loan, he may have been stuck with this loan in place until that loan term passed, which was six months!

When a loan turns from performing (the borrower pays as agreed) to non-performing (the borrower stops paying), it can be a stressful time for you as the lender. Try to keep emotion out of the decisions to move forward. Rely on the due diligence you did before the loan funded, including the rights you have as a lender to gain access to the collateral that secures your loan. Try to establish what the current situation is that caused the borrower financial hardship and assess if this is temporary or likely to continue to be a problem. Your personal timeline for the capital you deployed may be a consideration as well. Also, Carson's working with a borrower who didn't bury his head in the sand and make excuses helped tremendously. This is where having open lines of communication and getting a feel for your borrower's character can help avoid timely and costly processes that can ultimately harm both lender and borrower.

COLLECT & CONVEY IN REVIEW

C

COLLECT & CONVEY
You are almost across the finish line! The most rewarding part of the loan process is finally being able to sit back and collect interest payments. But there are still things to settle before you are completely done with the loan. First, you need to ensure project progress and timeliness of payments are continuing to happen. Be prepared for potential issues to arise that may require your involvement. Lastly, you need to ensure you get all your principal back, hopefully on time.

P

PERSON
This is when you and the borrower take over, unless you prefer to have a third-party servicer involved in collecting your monthly installment payments and providing end-of-year tax statements. Aside from you and the borrower, you may need to check in with contractors to ensure the project is running smoothly, should you want to participate in the project more actively.

PROPERTY
This is the time when you may choose to conduct site visits and ensure contractors and subs are being handled properly.

PAPERWORK
The paperwork here is monthly statements from the servicer, if used.

Other paperwork:
- 1098/1099-INT
- Lien-release waiver form
- Invoices (if holding money back for a rehab)

R

RISKS AND REWARDS
The temptation in this phase may be to sit back and watch the money roll in to your bank account, but failure to stay involved in the project progress or, at minimum, to ensure your loan payments are current could lead to big problems. Scheduling a regular check-in at least monthly can help to avoid any issues that may impact your lien position, your equity buffer, and the borrower's repayment plans (exit strategy).

CALL TO ACTION FOR COLLECT & CONVEY

After reading this chapter, you will need to:

1. Establish how payments will be made, either through a payment service or note servicing provider.
2. Set expectations for the type of communication, frequency of communication, and what information should be communicated to you as a lender from your borrower.
3. Have a payoff demand letter prepared according to the expected closing date for the sale or refinance of the property.
4. Have a satisfaction of mortgage or similar instrument drawn up and recorded after the loan has been repaid in full.

Chapter 9
UNDERWRITING DEEP DIVE— PERSON

There are a few different datapoints about the borrower you will want to review in more detail during the Compile & Condition step. After all, the borrower is the one who will be making the decisions about the property. In this chapter, we provide a baseline overview of the documents you may want to collect, as well as suggested follow-up conditions you could request if a document does not meet your standards on its own.

Understand that not all factors about the borrower will be quantitative when you review the documents. There are going to be qualitative characteristics that do not show up on paper, and it will be up to you to read between the lines. While we can point out some red flags we have seen and navigated during our own lending experiences, there are probably a plethora of other flags you may need to learn to recognize on your own as well.

If we're being honest, the only reason we are able to write this book and an entire chapter on underwriting is because we have experienced each issue firsthand and had to figure out the solutions in real time and on real deals. It's part of the risk involved in this type of investing. Just keep in mind that the skills and knowledge needed for underwriting can take a significant amount of time to develop. Only experience makes you better. Even then, you will never completely know the whole story. Your ultimate goal, therefore, will be to decide, with some level of certainty, what the probability will be for a positive, desired outcome—which is full repayment of your loan.

To do your due diligence on a loan requires you to become a detective. In the Compile & Condition step, your goal will be to find every reason to say no to the loan. This sounds counterintuitive but you need to be comfortable identifying all the potential issues and finding ways to solve those problems (through loan conditions) before you can proceed with the loan in good confidence.

As part of the underwriting deep dive, we will walk you through some of the most common documents requested by private lenders and what we look for when reviewing them. What we will not do, however, is provide you with the exact guidelines to assess a yes or no decision. Since we are not familiar with your state lending laws, your personal risk tolerance, and your preferred deal criteria established in the Calculate & Evaluate step, it'd be impossible for us to provide you with this type of decisioning tree.

What we will supply is what to look out for, key questions you should be able to answer, and some "if/then" statements that could support further conditioning of the loan. For example, if you find that the borrower resides at a property they do not currently own, then you might ask them about their past home ownership and why they chose to flip a house before establishing personal net worth. How you choose to evaluate their response and proceed is up to you.

VERIFYING YOUR BORROWER

As we mentioned in the Compile & Condition step, one commonly overlooked thing is verification that the person(s) you are lending to matches who (or what) will be purchasing the property. This may be a bit more complicated than just having a copy of their driver's license in your loan file. Purchasing a property requires the buyer to take the title to the property in some name and type of tenancy. Depending on the state, the spouse of a married borrower may have to sign the lien instrument or at minimum acknowledge the loan in some manner. Part of the title report will also include how the borrower will be taking the title to the property and if the borrower is married, divorced, legally separated, or single. Still request a copy of their identification showing name, address, and date of birth, but realize that is potentially just the tip of the iceberg.

Driver's License
When looking at photo identification for a potential borrower, you will want to look for a few things.
- Where does the borrower live, and do they own or rent? This can be cross-referenced using online public records on tax assessors' websites.

A concern about a borrower who is renting versus owning is the higher likelihood a renting borrower might move in to the property as their primary residence, while a borrower who currently owns and occupies their primary residence would be less likely to move. This is not always the case for borrowers renting versus owning, but it is something a lender should be mindful of when evaluating a lending opportunity.

- What is their legal full name, and does it match what is on the Purchase and Sale Agreement? People often go by different names so you need to take note of their legal name, which should be listed on legal documents.
- Full legal names are useful for background checks as well as inputting directly on your loan term sheet so that when you share this with your attorney for document drafting, it is entered appropriately.

Business-Entity Documents

Since we are private lenders who are also trying to stay in the business-purpose loan arena, we often lend to business entities. We previously mentioned that the types of business-entity documents you will need to collect depend on the type of business entity it is and in which state it was formed. Typically, however, you will be asking for either the Operating Agreement (for sole proprietorship, partnership, LLC) or Articles of Incorporation (for S corporations and C corporations) as well as a Certificate of Formation.

Corporations are generally more complex and structured and likely have the entity documents readily available upon request. In contrast, we find most smaller businesses and sole proprietorships are less organized, so receiving the required business-entity documents is frequently a challenge. We have encountered dozens of borrowers over the years who set up their business entities themselves either online or in person with the secretary of state. While there is nothing illegal about this do-it-yourself setup, it can be problematic when the documents required to obtain credit for the business have not yet been created—a common situation for single-member LLCs. The Operating Agreement will be a necessary document and you may have to pad some time into the transaction while the borrower gets this generated by an attorney.

Here are some additional steps to take when working with business-entity documents.

- Identify all the partners within the business entity and their respective percentage of membership.
- Identify which members are authorized signors, and which are not.

- Ensure the business is authorized to take out debt on behalf of the business entity.
- Is the person who manages the business entity actually your borrower? Make sure that those two names match.
- Make sure the business entity is active with the state.

We suggest that each member who has a 20 percent or greater ownership be a personal guarantor. Some borrowers will try to request only certain members be included in the loan, claiming they have sole rights to sign on behalf of the business. While that may be the case, we have been burned before by partnerships gone bad. In reality, Operating Agreements, particularly the Amendments that come after formation, are not a matter of public record, which could lead to issues after the loan is originated.

For example, we had a borrower (we'll call him Seth) who took out a loan against an industrial building in Seattle. The LLC was formed between Seth and another business partner who was not required to sign the loan. She was a silent-capital partner, and we knew Seth could handle the repositioning and selling of the building himself as a commercial broker. In the middle of the loan, we discovered the silent partner had started a lawsuit against Seth. It turns out that Seth had provided us with the original Operating Agreement showing he could sign on her behalf, but he did not supply us with the amendment signed by both parties six months after the original formation requiring her signatures in addition to Seth's on all loans, credit, and transfer-of-ownership documents. Fortunately, we were able to get paid off through a quick sale of the property, but the remaining net proceeds went into a trust account while the partners finished out their legal disputes with each other.

Business-entity documentation can be complex and confusing for the lay-person. We suggest you leave the hard work to the experts in this area. The two main issues you need to be concerned with as the lender are (1) the names of the members and reaching out to them directly, if possible, and (2) ensuring all member names with 20 percent or greater interest are included as personal guarantors. Other than that, any questions you may have with regards to the business entity should be left to your real estate attorney and the title department. A title officer is required to review business-entity documents and determine who is required to sign. They also validate if the business is active and ensure there are no liens against the business. When in doubt, have either or both of these two resources help you out, as needed.

Reaching out directly to all business members can also help catch some early inklings of partner disputes that may be brewing beneath the surface. Nothing can kill a business plan for a property faster than partnerships in the middle of a meltdown. If there are multiple partners on the Operating Agreement but one doesn't want to sign for the loan or provide a personal guarantee, that may be an early indication that there is trouble within that partnership structure. Alternatively, if the member you've been speaking to thus far refuses to provide partner contact information, that could also be a red flag.

EVALUATING THE EXPERIENCE OF THE BORROWER

Most private lenders only lend to borrowers who have some experience in real estate, specifically the type of project they are seeking funding for. What is considered "relevant experience" is completely up to you as the lender, but you will want to see a track record of successful completion of projects similar to the one you are considering lending on in the recent past and with their active participation.

For example, a borrower may be an "experienced" real estate investor because they have owned five other single-family homes as turnkey rentals for the past two years. This may not count as experience in your mind if the borrower is doing an extensive renovation on their latest purchase and looking to refinance after renovations are complete and a tenant has moved in to the home. Another one we see is general contractors who want to start flipping houses on their own. They may have extensive relevant experience but have not personally ever been on title on a project. It will be up to you to decide if that experience is enough or not. After all, completing the work is one hallmark of a successful flipper, but it's not the only one. The general contractor may understand operationally how to execute a rehab project but may not know anything about the acquisition, financial modeling, or sale of a flip.

Schedule of Real Estate Owned / Project Experience

When looking at the schedule of real estate owned you may come across different names your borrower has used, either personally or as a business. Using those names, you can search public records in that area for past properties they may not currently own. This can be especially helpful for borrowers who primarily use fix-and-flip as their business model for investing in real estate.

Their current schedule of real estate owned may not list any property other than their primary residence if they routinely work on one property at a time. You can ask the borrower for a list of past projects they have completed and sold as well. Searching public records will allow you to verify that they actually had the title to the properties they are claiming on their experience level, as well as verify the timeline during which they owned the property, the debt they had on the property, and the length of time they had that debt.

If they have used private loans or hard-money loans before, you should be able to see how long it took them to get in and out of the loan on that particular property. Many municipalities maintain public records through their clerk of court, who manages the database for online access. You may need to purchase access or copies of individual files if they are available online. These public records can show when the deed was signed over and when the owner took the title to the property through a recorded mortgage or deed of trust, which outlines the date, amount, and who the lender was. You can also see a satisfaction of mortgage for when that debt was paid off in public records.

Keep in mind that not all municipalities share public records online. Also, some records may be redacted, making it impossible to confirm persons, dates, and dollar amounts. If this happens, then you may want to request HUD-1 Closing Statements for their recent projects. Make sure it is the final settlement statement for when the borrower *sold* the property and not just when they *purchased* it. Even better, you can ask for both to show you the timeline of when the borrower purchased it and for how much, and when they sold it and for what price. What it does not tell you is how much the borrower spent in rehab costs, so determining a total project profit margin may be difficult.

The following are additional questions to consider when evaluating a current schedule of real estate owned and past projects.

- How much equity do they have in their existing rental portfolio? This is an indication of overall liquidity and net worth and measured by looking at the property debt versus estimated value. If your loan-to-value is too high for your comfort level, you could consider placing a lien against one of these properties in what is called a "cross-collateralization."
- How many projects have they done in the past?
- Is the borrower's name confirmed as a vested owner on these projects?
- Did the borrower work with other partners on these past projects and will those partners be participating on the new project?
- What are the reasons the borrower is not working with partners they've used in the past?
- If the borrower is working with a new partner, do they have anything in writing that outlines their roles, responsibilities, and capital contributions? This is commonly referred to as an "MOU," or "memo of understanding."

- If the borrower is using a new general contractor who has not worked on past projects, why?
- If the borrower says they did a majority of the work themselves on past projects, are they licensed, bonded, and insured?
- If the borrower has a W-2 day job, how often did they inspect or visit the jobsite in the past?
- Does the borrower have other projects going on simultaneously? Have they handled multiple projects at once before?
- Does the borrower have a full-time job and family obligations outside of this project? What are their plans for project management if they do?

If the borrower has a history of working with partners, then you will want to talk with your borrower to better understand the role each partner played, especially if the borrower is going out on their own this time. Then determine what competencies are being left on the table with these partners not in the picture. If the borrower is dismissive and tells you the partners provided very little in the way of support on these projects, you may want to dig a little deeper. Perhaps you contact some of the partners as a professional reference. What's more, if the partners were not listed as references, ask why. Partners who are purposefully omitted from the borrower's professional references list should give you a reason to probe a little further.

If you still want to lend to the individual who is doing much of the work themselves, you may want to build in some additional buffers to protect yourself, such as having them pay more up front in a down payment, building in prepaid interest for the length of the loan, having a longer-term loan, and incorporating very specific language in the documentation for the progress timeline of the project. That way, if things fall behind schedule, the loan can be in default and you, as the lender, can take over the project.

We've added a sample schedule of real estate/project experience in the supplemental materials at www.biggerpockets.com/lendingbonus.

Contacting Professional References

When you speak to the references, ask about their personal experiences with the borrower and in what capacity they have worked with the borrower. You can ask for specific addresses they may have partnered up with the borrower on in the past and how the borrower was involved. A quick public records search can verify if they were an actual partner vested on that property. This also helps you locate other current or past business entities that your borrower may be a member of.

Later, we will discuss how to validate the information you hear about in these meetings and calls. For now, just know what questions to ask, record what you hear, and make sure to set aside time after the discussion to do your own research. Each step of the lending process should follow this simple rule: Trust but verify.

Before ending a conversation with a reference, ask if they know of anyone else who has done business with the borrower. We call this "second-tier references." Those references are often where you get to the real story of what has been going on because they were not directly suggested by the borrower. Remember the conversation we had in the previous chapter about your reputation? Well, now you see why it is so important! Many people in real estate know a lot of other people in real estate. If you start burning bridges, it won't take long for others to see the smoke.

During your conversations with each of the references, you can also ask about the specific tasks your potential borrower had in relation to their business dealings. Try to establish what experience they have doing the type of project and handling the type of property they are seeking funding for now. If the borrower was a capital partner to someone else and the personal reference actually handled the day-to-day decisions of the renovation but was not involved in the subject property renovations, this may be a cause for increasing the rate of the loan or denying the loan if you feel the borrower is not able to perform alone, either due to lack of experience or time commitments elsewhere in their life.

If you talk with some of the professional references supplied to you and you still feel comfortable moving forward to the next steps, then you can progress to gathering additional paperwork to get a better feel for this loan and to get some more details down on paper.

EVALUATING THE BORROWER'S CHARACTER

During the Contact step, we gave you some pointers for getting to know the potential borrower. Beyond the initial meet and greet, there are a few things you can do to investigate the borrower—both their background and their online presence.

Background Searches

Not all lenders choose to do official background checks. On the borrower 1003 application, there is a question regarding past felonies. If it's checked, then you may want to do a background search or simply ask the borrower to explain the circumstances. How much do you really care if the woman in her 30s received a "minor in possession" charge as a kid? If the question about felonies is unchecked, then perhaps you do not proceed with a background check. It is completely up to you, but here are a few things we would want to know about.

- Past convictions related to bankruptcy, fraud, or theft that pose financial risk
- Violent crimes, which would be a personal-safety concern
- History of litigation and summary judgments against the borrower, which could be indicative of litigious behavior

Aside from the obvious financial and personal-safety risks, one issue with past felony convictions is the borrower could have a harder time obtaining conventional financing, should they decide to turn the property into a rental rather than put it back on the market. We personally believe most people deserve second chances and have chosen to originate loans to borrowers with past criminal records. It will be up to you to determine how concerning the past prior convictions are to the overall success of the project and full repayment of your loan.

There are many ways to do a character evaluation.

- **Basic:** Do an online search of the borrower name(s) and/or business entities. Be sure to check out any social media pages they have set up. Web searches can often pull up litigation, court cases, and news articles related to the person. This is the most basic and easiest option but may not pull up detailed results.
- **Intermediate:** Public Access to Court Electronic Records (PACER) service provides electronic public access to federal court records. It gives the public instantaneous access to more than one billion documents filed at all federal courts. This is little to no cost depending on the results pulled, but it can be a little tricky to figure out the best way to conduct your online searches and may require some playing around. The PACER site is located at: pacer.uscourts.gov.
- **Advanced:** If you are a landlord and use online tools to conduct background checks on tenants, you could use these same tools for your prospective borrowers. Be sure to check with your local real estate attorney on the legality of conducting searches as a lender and not a landlord. You will need to ensure you are legally conducting a background check and receiving authorization as required by your state regulations, if any.

Social Media and Online Presence

You can dig into their social media presence to see what kind of activities or topics the potential borrower chooses to share. An easy first step is asking to be a connection on whatever social media platform you choose. Scroll through to see where they are posting from and what topics and photos they choose to share. This can give you some insight into the type of person the borrower may be when they aren't on their "first date" best behavior while you two have coffee one morning. Another tried-and-true method is simply looking up their name on any major search engine and any business entities they may operate. Here are some things to consider.

- How do you feel about what they share with the world?
- Do they brag about getting away with things? For example, have they advertised a loan modification and the fact that they now owe less on a property, making it a "home run deal?" (This is an actual example we've experienced.)
- What can you glean about their real estate experience? Real estate investors are typically boastful about their completed projects, which can further validate their experience (or not).
- Do they have a ton of travel posts throughout the year, making you wonder what time they have for a new project?

Be Fair and Consistent

When evaluating a person's character, remember that much of your sleuthing may be more qualitative than quantitative and can leave room for ambiguity and potential liability. You therefore need to have some written policies or procedures in place for evaluating a borrower. Discrimination against a borrower based on a protected class can really damage your reputation as a lender. Plus, it's illegal. You want to try to have similar underwriting standards for each potential new loan and have some metrics that may make a no to a loan more quantitative than qualitative, should a discrimination accusation come your way as a lender.

As you move through loan opportunities, make it a practice to go back over files and evaluate why you turned a file down and document that information. Making this type of review part of your normal lending practice as you grow will be vital. While you may never intend to discriminate, you may be putting parameters in place that do not give all borrowers an equal opportunity to meet those guidelines, or worse, you may be putting a different set of guidelines on a borrower or a property because of the location (side of town, rental rates versus home ownership rates, etc.), or requiring a borrower from a protected class to have more experience or more assets compared to another borrower. Discrimination is not to be tolerated. Keeping that at the forefront in your lending practices will go a long way toward building your credibility as a lender, as well as keep you out of hot water should litigation happen. We suggest having a conversation with your real estate attorney on how to avoid discrimination accusations and what you can do in your underwriting practices to be fair, consistent, and legally safeguarded at all times.

EVALUATING THE BORROWER'S CAPACITY

Liquid Assets

The first capacity many lenders are interested in is the asset levels the borrower has at the time of application. Statements from bank accounts, certificates of deposit, money market accounts, equities accounts, and retirement accounts are usually supplied by the borrower. Evaluating the borrower's liquid assets is critical for two reasons: (1) they indicate if the borrower has the funds to bring cash to close at the time of purchase, and (2) they tell you if the borrower has enough funds to cover their out-of-pocket expenses related to the project, such as rehab and monthly carrying costs.

When addressing the borrower's capacity, how much is too much? Sure, the banks may require a lot more proof in the way of liquidity, but they are also going to enter into a thirty-year loan with the borrower. You are not. In a short-term circumstance, your qualifications should be considerably less substantial. That said, you want to ensure your borrower has a decent net worth in case they do not perform, though this can also be easily safeguarded by the equity buffer in the property as opposed to a person's net worth.

In theory, personal net worth is a strong indication a borrower could potentially liquidate assets to pay off your loan. In reality, many borrowers who experience issues on projects or stop performing altogether will not liquidate a performing portfolio of liquid assets to pay off the lender. You will therefore still need to go into a foreclosure as a way to repossess the property, sell it at auction, and recoup your principal investment. Realistically, you will not be able to go after the borrower's liquid assets using a property foreclosure proceeding either.

When evaluating a borrower's liquid assets, these are the types of accounts to consider, in order of importance:
- Personal and business bank depository accounts
- Home equity and other lines of credit opened (could be an asset when not drawn against)
- Stocks, certificates of deposit, funds, and other assets
- Retirement plans, annuities, cash-value life insurance, etc.

We believe that bank accounts and untapped lines of credit are the easiest to liquidate should things go wrong and a borrower need access to funds quickly and without penalty. The latter two have adjustable valuations and can be liquidated but at a cost, either through penalties, capital gains (if any), interest, or taxes. All that said, when looking at liquid assets from your borrower, it's important to figure out how to ask for "just enough." Striking a healthy balance will be critical here.

Note that while there may be considerable assets in retirement accounts, they are often protected from asset seizures in legal proceedings, such as foreclosure and judgments due to deficiency of the property to satisfy the outstanding balance. In addition, some accounts may fluctuate greatly, depending on the overall market. Think of a stock portfolio and how the prices of those underlying securities can change minute to minute during a trading day. Some lenders may only consider about 70 percent of the balance in these types of accounts to compensate for the volatility of the account. Another option is to use the average value of the account over a period of time if there have been large gains or losses due to the assets being held.

These accounts should have monthly or quarterly statements provided to the borrower. When reviewing these statements, check the date of the statement balance, the borrower's name, address on the statement, and that all pages of the statement were submitted. If you have a borrower who does not have regular income, such as a paycheck from a W-2 job, you may need two to six months at a minimum to establish the amount of income the borrower gets over time.

Here are some additional questions to ask when reviewing bank statements.
- How much are the balances being held in the account?
- Does the account have enough funds to cover the amount needed to close on the transaction? If not, ask for statements for the account where the funds will be wired from.
- Does the borrower have a history of poor cash management? If you see several overdraft fees, it could be an indication that the borrower is not paying close enough attention to their finances, which can include the interest-only payments to you, the lender.
- Does the borrower have sufficient cash reserves needed to refinance? Sometimes borrowers decide to keep the flip as a rental (or are forced to due to market constraints) and will need cash reserves to qualify for a refinance. If not, does the borrower have sufficient income levels to create cash reserves in a relatively short amount of time?

You are trying to establish if the borrower has enough in liquid assets for the costs associated with both acquiring and executing the business plan for the property. Your comfort level with the amount of capital you want a borrower to have depends on your risk tolerance, exit strategy planned for the borrower, potential equity in another property the borrower owns, how much debt the borrower is personally responsible for each month, and the ease of access to that capital. At every step, you need to ask yourself, "What will I do if my borrower doesn't pay me?" If you have a good answer, then the borrower's money management history becomes less important.

We are often asked how much capital a borrower should have, and the answer, as usual, is "it depends." If you are really concerned with the borrower's ability to qualify for a refinance, you could have the borrower get a pre-approval letter from a lender stating the requirements the borrower must meet, such as length of ownership of the property and condition of the property, asset levels and credit score requirements, and upper limit of debt-to-income ratio. However, if the primary goal is to sell the property once the renovations are completed, then proof of enough funds to cover all the borrower's out-of-pocket expenses should suffice.

Income Level

To further assess the capacity (one of the C's of underwriting) of a borrower to pay the obligations of this new loan, you should look at the borrower's income level. This can quickly become a very complex topic, especially if you have multiple borrowers. Depending on the situation, there are various pieces of documentation to ask for if you are concerned about the income of the borrower.

First you need to decide how much you care about income source and cash flow. Some lenders want proof of employment and like to see steady, high income salaries. Others tend to view day jobs as an impediment to completing real estate projects in a timely manner. If you have enough equity in the project as is, perhaps add prepaid interest payments or defer all monthly payments to the end of the loan term so the borrower doesn't have to worry about monthly interest payments. Or if the borrower has a boatload of cash in their account, decide how much you care about monthly income produced by the borrower. This way, you do not have to look into the borrower's employment history and income levels as intensely, if at all.

From another perspective, borrowers seeking private financing often prefer it to conventional financing—not just for speed but for the ease of acquiring credit. Less stringent qualification requirements and lower documentation needs make it ideal for a busy flipper wearing multiple hats and trying to keep things as simple as possible on a short-term loan. If your document requests start looking like that of a bank with lots of personal-income documentation, they may choose to go to another private lender with fewer requirements.

We are not telling you to abandon efforts to inquire about a borrower's financial welfare, but you will need to strike a balance between asking for just enough to give you a reasonable storyline and not overburdening the borrower with unnecessary personal and financial invasion.

If you choose to evaluate a borrower's source of income, you may wish to evaluate it from two angles: monthly and annually. One offers insight into current income levels while the other gives a stronger sense of historical income levels. Both are necessary to determine the strength of the borrower's income stream in terms of overall earning potential and reliability of various income sources.

Monthly income sources include:

- **W-2 income:** Ask for two months of pay stubs or direct deposits into a bank account to show recent earned income.
- **Self-employed:** If they are a W-2 earner, you can ask for the same as above, as well as a year-to-date Profit and Loss Statement (YTD P&L).
- **Rental income:** Ask for two months of bank deposits showing rent deposits.

Annual income sources include:

- **W-2 income:** Ask for one or two years' worth of W-2s to show overall income earned.
- **Self-employed:** Ask for two years' worth of Schedule C income on the borrower's tax returns and K-1s.
- **Rental income:** Ask for a year-to-date Profit and Loss Statement and one or two prior years' worth. You could also request Schedule E portions of recent tax returns showing rental income reported; however, real estate investors often take considerable deductions and depreciation, which may make it more difficult to ascertain simple property cash flow.

Here are a few more questions to ask when reviewing a borrower's income sources and levels.

- Does the borrower have sufficient means to make the monthly interest payments? This is the most critical question you are trying to answer and why monthly cash flow is important.
- Would the borrower be able to qualify for a mortgage to refinance the loan should they want or need to turn it into a rental property instead of flipping it?

- Does the borrower have steady employment history? This often says more about character than financial stability.
- If you have a difficult time establishing how much income is sufficient, are there easier ways to underwrite the borrower or modify loan terms to accommodate this lack of personal knowledge?
- What field do they currently work in?
- How could the borrower's income be impacted by an economic downturn, an advancement in technology, or a federal or state regulation change?

EVALUATING THE BORROWER'S CREDIT HISTORY

IMPORTANT: You will be required to have borrower consent, in writing, in order to run a credit check.

Credit reports are often used as a way for lenders to assess the borrower's likelihood of execution based on past performance. While this is a key metric for financial institutions that extend credit and long-term loans, such as thirty-year loans, your loan will be for a much shorter duration, so your credit requirements should probably be far less rigorous, especially if you are not well-versed in what to look for as a lender. We'll provide you with an overview of what to look out for, where to look for credit, and how to perform a basic credit analysis so you can add this to your overall borrower storyline and move on to the next piece of underwriting.

There are many different ways to do a credit analysis.

- **Basic:** Have a borrower send you a screenshot of their free credit score through one of their banking apps or have them create a free account on www.freecreditreport.com
- **Intermediate:** Have the borrower run a free credit report and send you a copy of it
- **Advanced:** Run your own credit report (either soft or hard) using companies who provide this service to landlords

The basic FICO scores range from a low of 300 to a high of 850. Here is a general breakdown.

- **Excellent:** 750 to 850
- **Good:** 700 to 749
- **Fair:** 650 to 699
- **Poor:** 550 to 649
- **Very poor:** 300 to 549

When evaluating a borrower's credit, consider the following:

- Is the credit score in the range to qualify for a refinance? (Generally, 660 and above meet minimum thresholds and 740 or more qualifies for the best rates, even with many hard-money lenders.)
- Where is the credit score coming from?
- What is the borrower's reason for a low score? Is it from just a few missed payments or a bankruptcy? The explanation can often be more telling than the score itself.
- What blemishes on the credit stand out? Is there a large volume of past due, late payments, or delinquent accounts?
- Does the borrower have minimal credit? This may result in an artificially low score, so looking at score alone may not be a good gauge in determining creditworthiness.

If you deny the loan application due to findings from the credit report, you will need to notify the borrower in writing on the loan decision and why it was declined.

Another limitation of pulling a personal credit report is that any credit taken out in a business name that a borrower may be personally liable for may not appear on the credit report. You may see an inquiry, but you won't see the corresponding debt account, if one was granted.

One metric you may use to evaluate when looking at the credit report is the borrower's debt-to-income ratio (DTI). The borrower's DTI is a percentage that tells lenders how much income they bring in versus how much they need to pay in debt service. You can calculate the DTI by adding up the borrower's monthly minimum debt payments and dividing that sum by their monthly pretax income. If the borrower wants to refinance your private mortgage into conventional lending, the underwriter will examine the borrower's existing debts and compare them to their income to ensure the borrower has sufficient cash flow to cover their monthly mortgage payments, taxes, and insurance.

If you would rather not deal with pulling credit on a potential borrower, you can instead request statements for debt accounts that might be of interest. For example, mortgage statements provided by the borrower contain valuable information. Fortunately, there is industry uniformity across the range of mortgage statements from different lenders. This is because the Dodd-Frank Act, passed in the wake of the 2008 financial crisis, requires mortgage servicers to follow a standardized model for mortgage statements highlighting specific loan information. Look at the property address on the statements and double-check if they appear on the SREO. You will also want to compare the address on the statement with the address of the property that the mortgage statement covers. The address of the borrower and the subject property need to be different. If they're the same, it's an owner-occupied property. Remember, you *do not* want to lend on owner-occupied properties. You only want to lend on non-owner-occupied property.

You'll also want to pay particular attention to the amount of the monthly payment, the outstanding principal on the loan, taxes and insurance, and any delinquencies or late fees. If a borrower has had trouble making mortgage payments to other lenders, it may be a red flag for this new mortgage they are trying to obtain from you.

Pledge of Ownership Shares

If the business entity will be on the title and deed to the property, the owners can offer an ownership pledge of the entity—in other words, put up the business as additional collateral. You would do this through a process known as a UCC filing. UCC stands for Uniform Commercial Code. UCC allows for a blanket lien, which gives a creditor (you, the lender) an interest in any assets that business entity owns. Individual states may have different processes for the UCC filing, so check into that process if this is something you are considering doing as a lender.

Here are some other things to keep in mind for UCC filings.

- The lien is only as good as the valuation of the company. Most sole proprietorships or partnerships have little in assets or revenue to substantiate the need for a business lien.
- They are typically only done on well-established businesses with reliable sources of revenue from which to recoup your investment or with assets such as heavy machinery, fleet vehicles, real estate, or other liquid assets that could be repossessed.

At a high level, a UCC lien allows you to gain ownership of the business entity that owns the property ,and hold what is termed a "UCC sale." A UCC sale typically takes one to two months, so it will likely be faster than most traditional foreclosure processes. You as the lender end up taking ownership control of the "borrower," which is the business entity.

The challenge with this method is that many title companies may want to see an actual foreclosure proceeding to get clear title on the property when you, as a lender, decide to sell the property. In a way, you would have to foreclose on yourself as that business entity, but given that it would be uncontested, it would make the foreclosure process more streamlined and allow you to have ownership of the asset sooner, mitigating your risk of vengeful damage to the property.

A UCC lien is generally something you can ask for to help mitigate the risk in a loan, possibly with a new or inexperienced investor. It allows you as the lender to regain physical control of the property quickly so work can continue on the property even while foreclosure proceedings are clearing up the title for an eventual sale. Again, consult with an attorney familiar in lending to ask about this option and what the pros and cons might be to include this under certain circumstances. Some borrowers may outright refuse to pursue this option, as they may hold multiple properties in the borrowing entity and may be unwilling to put their entire portfolio at risk for this one property. If this is the case, clauses can be added to outline that certain assets are exempt from this arrangement if the remaining assets are more than enough to cover the debt. Much like the person-guaranty process, you can choose when and if you want to include this as an option to mitigate your risk.

OTHER BORROWER ISSUES

During negotiations, some danger signs may appear. You may choose to overlook them or demand clarification from the applicant. Some of the red flags exist only in your own mind—beware of them!

"I Know the Borrower, and Therefore I Trust Them."

That's fine, but business is business. Even if you have known your best friend for decades, we doubt you know their credit score or how much they owe on their vehicles. Your contract with your friend must be identical to a contract you'd write with a stranger. It must be crystal clear and fair to both sides. A handshake is no substitute for a signature! For this very reason, we tend to avoid doing business with personal friends. It gets too sticky.

Poor History of Paying Back Creditors

If your borrower can't or won't pay others what they owe them, why should you be any different? Loan modifications, short sales, and credit forgiveness are all signs to look out for from a borrower who does not always seem compelled to own their financial obligations.

Cannot Answer Questions about the Project

Hope is not a strategy! Your borrower needs to have a clear plan that they can show you and discuss.

What's Said Isn't What's Written

It doesn't matter what your borrower says. All that matters is the facts written in the documents and in the contract. Reading between the lines, if what they tell you does not match what they have on paper, then it's an issue of trustworthiness.

Borrower Desperation

You want a borrower who's responsive and communicative. If your borrower seems desperate, in a hurry, or overly anxious, you should step back and dig deeper. Perhaps every other lender has turned them down because they've seen something you're missing. At the end of the day, people who are financially well-organized are not waiting until the last minute and desperate for a loan. Or the borrower may simply be high-maintenance and require constant and tiresome babysitting.

Chapter 10
UNDERWRITING DEEP DIVE— PROPERTY

The property is the collateral used to secure the loan. Some lenders like to focus more on the borrower and less on the property, or vice versa. One school of thought believes the borrower oversees everything and is the material participant, which is true. Properties don't pay their own bills; people do. However, the other school of thought places more value in the borrower's equity on the property, as this is the single biggest protection on your loan. The size of the equity buffer and the resale value is critical to recovering your principal loan amount as well as any interest and legal fees should something go wrong. The bigger the equity protection on the subject property, the less you have to be concerned with the activities of the borrower.

No matter where you sit on this spectrum, underwriting both aspects thoroughly and properly is important because it's difficult to have a successful transaction without both running smoothly. Yes, the borrower will be the one making the decisions on behalf of the property, but the numbers for the property also need to be within your lending parameters.

In our pre-step, Calculate & Evaluate, you looked at lending criteria before you even started talking to people about lending. In this chapter, we are going to do more analysis of loan terms that you may want to consider with each potential lending opportunity based on your own risk tolerance. Another way to develop your own framework is to reach out to other lenders to ask about their lending criteria and why they have certain ones in place. Keep in mind that you will need to weigh the uniqueness of each lending opportunity to make sure that the risk you are bearing as a lender is accounted for with each new circumstance. Having a general framework and knowing why you have it can help guide you toward a yes, no, or maybe on a loan and help you decide under what terms.

Finally, we will introduce some additional lending criteria that you may want to add to a specific loan or every loan, depending on your business model. We will also look at different ways to establish the value of the collateral.

DEAL ANALYSIS AND PROPERTY DUE DILIGENCE

It is worth repeating that the way in which a lender underwrites a loan opportunity on a fix-and-flip is very similar to how a borrower completes their deal analysis as the investor. In fact, many of the same principles and datapoints are used by both.

While we will cover some of the key terms you will need to use in your property valuations and loan due diligence, remember that you will also need to hone your knowledge of how investors review fix-and-flip opportunities. This can be done through other real estate investing resources readily available to you. Check out the resources at www.biggerpockets.com/lendingbonus for some suggestions and recommendations.

PROPERTY VALUATIONS

There are a variety of ways to have an as-is and ARV established for you, but keep in mind that the value is an estimate and can vary depending on who you ask or where you are obtaining your information.

The following property valuation options are listed in order of most complex, costly, and time-consuming to easiest and lowest cost:

1. Appraisals

These must be completed by an appraisal management company (AMC) complying with Uniform Standards of Professional Appraisal Practice (USPAP) and law. Licensed and trained appraisers will complete a site visit and conduct research to assess a property's current value (and potentially ARV) and, generally speaking, will adjust values up and down based on dissimilarities like no garage, below-grade square footage (basements), and traffic.

The major drawback to a full appraisal is the time and the cost. Investors often want to use a private lender for speed and ease of obtaining the loan.

Appraisals can take weeks to schedule and as a private lender, it can be extremely difficult to find one willing to work with you on a one-off basis, since they typically get most of their business through relationships with banks and other larger lending institutions. This time delay (and cost) goes against the borrower's primary reason for using private money in the first place. Because of this, most lenders will choose an alternative to obtaining a full appraisal.

2. Broker Price Opinion

BPOs are typically quicker, less involved, and not completed by a licensed appraiser. They are therefore not subject to the rigid USPAP guidelines. Since they can be done by professionals who are not appraisers, the timeline for completing a BPO is much quicker, typically less than two weeks. However, the reports may not be quite as thorough as a full appraisal. BPOs can often be completed either as a drive-by (exterior only) or through an interior walk-through.

3. Comparative Market Analysis

CMAs generally come from a real estate agent or broker. These reports are based off data available on the MLS for recently sold properties. Keep in mind that most real estate agents make their money from commissions, and the few hundred bucks collected on a CMA will likely not be very attractive. We have not had much luck obtaining CMAs unless the agent has already been promised the property "list back." In other words, they are going to list the property for your borrower once the renovation is complete.

4. Hybrid Valuation Tools and Automated Valuation Models (AVMs)

There has been a lot of innovation in the real estate valuation industry. With a little know-how and online access, many lenders are opting to do their own internal valuations. AVMs are, as the name implies, an automated way to achieve a ballpark valuation very quickly through online databases and mathematical algorithms. Some lenders like the ease and speed of AVMs, while others question the results and feel that machines can't always provide the level of analysis needed compared to the human eye.

Lenders skeptical of AVMs prefer using these databases themselves and narrowing down the criteria, location, and other property factors as they see fit. There are minimal charges for these reports, and they let you customize a variety of criteria that make results stronger. For example, if you live across the street from the water, you can draw a line to exclude any waterfront properties. This type of analysis can be great for private lenders with a little real estate market understanding. Plus, the results are much stronger than Zestimates and other valuation estimates found online, such as Redfin.

Speaking of Zillow and Redfin, both websites have the ability to show you recently sold homes, which can be helpful with your initial online research. When you type in an address for the subject property on Redfin, for example, the bottom of the property page will list Nearby Recently Sold Homes. You will have to do your own work to distill which are similar and which are not.

To learn more about online valuation solutions, check out the resources at www.biggerpockets.com/lendingbonus.

ASSESSING THE PROJECT SCOPE OF WORK

The scope of work is an itemized list of repairs or additions that the borrower plans to perform on the property, including estimates for costs. Those rehab estimates may be from bids the borrower already has on the property or just a guess of what the cost will be based on previous experience. The key action items when reviewing a scope of work are establishing if those costs are reasonable and if the scope of work matches up with what is needed for the property. Reading through the scope of work can be a bit daunting, which is why it is best to start with a conversation with the borrower about what they plan on doing to the property while looking at the scope of work during the conversation. You are not trying to nail down the cost of everything to the penny, but it is crucial to establish a general idea of what some of the costs are likely to be, especially if you are dealing with a property that may not have a large equity buffer (colloquially called a "thin deal"), a borrower who is short on capital to pay for repairs, or a borrower who is inexperienced.

Here are some additional considerations to keep in mind when reviewing the rehab budget.

- Are the estimates reasonable or do some seem low?
- Are there items missing from the list like hardware, lighting, and mill-work? Use a rehab calculator, such as the BiggerPockets rehab estimator (www.biggerpockets.com/rehab-estimator) to generate a report and gut-check that the budget is inclusive and accurate.
- Does the rehab budget have a reasonable contingency? This is a placeholder for budget overruns and is usually around 10 percent of the total costs.
- If they plan to do a kitchen or bathroom remodel, are there line items for new plumbing and electrical?

- Are subcontractors listed by each line item so you know who will be doing what? Beware the investor who thinks they'll be ripping and replacing all the plumbing themselves, unless they're a licensed plumber.
- What permits will be needed and who will be responsible for obtaining them?

Digging into the scope of work like this can unearth some other issues the borrower may not have thought about, or it might bring to light problems you overlooked in other parts of the underwriting process.

You may feel unfit to do a thorough review of the rehab plan. If this is the case, there are many resources available—from books to online forums—to give you an idea of what various repairs cost. If you have questions, ask. Join local groups on social media centered around real estate or repair work and ask if an amount is reasonable for this type of repair in the area. There is also a book on estimating rehab budgets available through BiggerPockets that could prove to be a helpful guide. Guess what it's called? *The Book on Estimating Rehab Costs* by J Scott!

You can also start building a network of contractors from various specialties and ask them about prices of items. While you may not be able to run through everything line by line with them on every deal, it can help you to get contacts in the area should your borrower need the additional support during the loan process. You could even pay a contractor (or retired contractor) a nominal fee to review scopes of work for you and to do follow-up inspections as work progresses to make sure the work the borrower says is complete is actually done and to code.

Other than establishing if the costs are reasonable, the other thing to consider with the scope of work is the timeline these renovations will take. This can be very different from project to project. Also, if the borrower is planning to do some of the work themselves, their timeline may be longer than a professional in that field.

Here are some additional questions to consider around the project timeline.
- Is the estimated time frame reasonable?
- Has the borrower secured bids from contractors so they can be placed on their schedule?
- What are the permits required for the scope of work and how long does it take to schedule and pass an inspection?
- What is the median home price in this market and what are the average days on market (DOM) for a property of this size and ARV?

- Is the borrower planning to be the general contractor (GC) on the project or have they engaged with someone who will act in this capacity? (If they plan to be their own GC, many municipalities require a license. If borrower plans to hire one, make sure they are licensed, bonded, and insured.)

As you do more loans in a particular market, you will start to learn more about vendors in the area. This information is invaluable, as a future borrower may say they are going to use a certain vendor, but your experience might have been that they are terribly slow. You can then inform the borrower of this and have them adjust their timeline, expectations, or choice of vendor.

Also take into account the total timeline and when the borrower may have a property going to market. Traditional buying seasons exist in most of the country, and the real estate sales market may slow down in winter months, with fewer buyers actively in the market during the holidays. The property may also not sell for as much as it would during the more in-demand season (usually April through August in the U.S.). That timeline could ultimately affect the value of the home, so be sure to look at the scope of work and how long the planned renovations are slated to take if the borrower purchases the property toward the end of the buying season or beginning of the off-peak season.

Another renovation timeline consideration is the availability of vendors and supplies to complete the required renovations. Some vendors in an area may be backlogged for work for weeks or months. This can be especially true in smaller metro areas or rural regions where there is a limited number of options for vendors. The borrower may have to pay additional charges to bring in a vendor from outside the area to complete the work. Furthermore, the global pandemic has stressed supply chains across the globe. Even though a product may be made in the U.S. or even in the borrower's own hometown, chances are that product relies on other items from around the globe. During 2020, the U.S. saw shortages in basic building materials like wood and cement, with a drastic increase in cost to go along with it. Being aware of these changes and having the borrower build in some slack for overages into the budget will help keep everyone prepared should something happen during renovations. Even in larger metro areas, it is worth a quick phone call to any vendors the borrower plans to use to see if there are any current lag times before work can begin. The borrower may not have a specific vendor selected yet, but proactively contacting a few different vendors to get the pulse of what is going on in the local market (lead times, average costs, etc.) may help give you insights into potential problems before they develop.

Lastly, recognize you will need to seek out more information and support to understand how to assess a fix-and-flip project. As mentioned earlier, the datapoints are similar for both borrower and lender. If we tried to impart everything there is to know about flipping, it would be an entire book. (In fact, it already is its own book. Just check out J Scott's other book, *The Book on Flipping Houses*.) The few metrics and considerations we shared with you here are just the foundational questions to pose. You will have to dig in deeper and with each deal, you will be able to underwrite the deal more quickly and more thoroughly.

PROPERTY VALUATION METRICS

Loan-to-Value Metrics

The loan-to-value (LTV) metric is the one most often quoted when lenders and borrowers first start talking about a lending opportunity. The lower the LTV you are lending on, the "safer" the loan is deemed, as it ensures you will have substantial equity in the property should you need to foreclose. That means the property could be liquidated at public auction, if you must foreclose, for at least what you are owed, including the principal amount, interest, and default interest owed, late fees, or legal fees associated with the foreclosure process.

Lenders use metrics like LTV to help determine how much the loan amount should be and how the loan should be structured based on the amount of capital the borrower has to infuse into the project. For a vanilla cosmetic rehab fix-and-flip project where no major capital improvements or structural repairs, additions, etc. will be taking place, you will want to create your loan amount based on the LTV and/or LT-ARV.

Loan-to-values can be presented in a few different ways, the most common being:

- **Loan-to-as-is-value (LTV):** What is the loan amount compared to the current property value?
- **Loan-to-after-repair-value (LT-ARV):** What is the loan amount compared to the renovated property value?
- **Loan-to-cost (LTC):** What is the loan amount compared to the total project costs, including acquisition, carry costs, and sale costs?

As-Is Value vs. After-Repair Value

The first metric to look at is the as-is value of the property. The simplest way to represent this would be based on the purchase price. However, some borrowers can find great deals where they have "walk-in" equity, or instant equity, due to the purchase price being below market value. Conversely, competition in stiff markets can make some purchases exceed fair market value. Example: If your loan amount is $100,000 and the purchase price is $150,000, your LTV is 66 percent (100,000 / 150,000 = .66).

ARV is the perceived market value of the property once it's completely renovated. It is represented by more of a projected range than a solid number and can be a moving target, while as-is value is more stable and precise. Understanding both the as-is value as well as the ARV is needed to assess the overall health of a project plan and to ensure the borrower will be able to make reasonable profit margins. For a more conservative valuation, the as-is value can be used instead of the ARV, which can keep you from lending too much money on a property in its current state. Example: If your loan amount is $100,000 and the resale price (ARV) is $300,000, your LT-ARV is 33 percent (100,000 / 300,000 = .33).

Structuring private loans is like the thirty-one flavors at Baskin Robbins. The choices are plentiful, so it makes explaining the "how" of tailoring your loan terms a little difficult. Just remember that as a beginner, you will want to start off slow and easy. The most basic of lending terms is to lend at a conservative percentage of the purchase price (assuming the purchase price does not exceed as-is market value) and then make the borrower bring down payment funds to close and fund their entire rehab.

You might think this is a near impossible scenario, but it does exist out there. We have borrowers requesting loans at 75 percent LTV all the time, and they will bring 25 percent to close as well as fund their entire rehab. Flippers need to manage the financials of their projects to make sure they hit target profit margins. That said, there is a balance between getting too much leverage (debt) at a high interest rate and keeping capital liquid in their accounts. Yet conservative LTV loans do exist out there and we encourage you to find a no-brainer deal like this to start your private lending journey, even if you have to lower your interest rates to be more attractive since these deals often have more competition than higher-risk loans. After this one, or perhaps a few more, then you can take the training wheels off. Of course, if you are seasoned in real estate investing and understand the key financials of a fix-and-flip property, you may understand your risks a little more and choose not to go this more conservative route. As always, the choice is yours.

In times of uncertainty, lenders will traditionally become more conservative in their valuations and will lower the LTV on which they are willing to lend. A lender may have typically funded at 75 percent LTV, but many during the pandemic quickly lowered that amount, sometimes to as low as 50 percent. Like many things in lending, there is a balance between what the market is offering a borrower and where you feel safe as a lender of your own capital. As a lender, you can change the terms of subsequent loans with the same borrower. We have said that the first loan is going to be the "most expensive" because you do not have any track record with that borrower. Later, if they need another loan for their next investment purchase, and if they had a good record of payment and communication on the first loan, then you might feel more secure with that loan because of the successful history. Each lending opportunity should be weighed individually, but having a strong track record with previous loans can be a good indication that they will continue to work well to complete the project and pay you monthly (getting you all of your capital back). These earlier lending opportunities with the same borrower can have more safeguards in place, such as lower LTC or LTV, and more conservative valuations for the ARV.

Some lenders choose to lend only on the as-is value of the property as it currently stands without any renovations. The as-is value is especially important if the property needs a significant amount of renovation. You do not want to lend $100,000 on a property that, in reality, may only be worth $70,000 in its current condition because it has major structural damage, water damage, fire damage, or foundation issues. If the borrower defaults on the loan before the renovations are complete, you will be stuck with a loan for significantly more than the property could be liquidated for at an auction. This is very bad for you as the lender because you will likely lose money unless you have additional funds to complete the renovations and put it back on the market for resale. We've heard many stories from lenders stuck in this predicament who had to flip a house themselves to secure their principal investment of capital.

You will also want to look at comparable properties to establish the amenities and quality of finishes they have compared to the borrower's expected rehab plans. Over-improving a property will generally not lead to a dollar-for-dollar improvement in the value of a home. The ARV can be different, depending on the scope of work the borrower plans to do with a property. Some repairs will improve the value of the property for the cost of renovations or more, such as remodeling and updating kitchens and bathrooms. Other renovations or updates may add little to no value to the property, but may be required as part of the renovation process for curb appeal, or required by current building codes to be updated. If the borrower spends $10,000 putting in a new driveway but cuts corners in a kitchen remodeling, they are not likely to raise the value of the home by $10,000, as new driveways don't necessarily add value to a home, whereas a completely redone kitchen does. The ARV will depend somewhat on those budget allocations made by the borrower, who will be actively managing this project. Lending based on ARV is frequently done, so what the property could sell for with the renovations planned is a critical metric to understand as the lender. You can always seek help and input along the way, which we will discuss next, but realize that, as mentioned earlier, ARV is a range, not an exact number, and could vary by 5 to 10 percent. Many investors have been surprised by appraisals at the refinancing point that have either come in too low or higher than expected.

Loan-to-Cost

The loan-to-cost is a slightly different beast. It measures the loan amount against the total project costs. This is a metric of how much you are willing to lend compared to the cost of acquisition plus renovation costs. This should be a metric found on the borrower's project pro forma. You will most certainly want to vet out the numbers provided by the borrower, but it's a good place to start with your analysis.

Lending on an LTC basis can ensure that a borrower has some of their own capital in the deal—both as part of the down payment as well as contributing their own funds to the project costs. Theoretically they are less likely to walk away when the going gets tough. It can also help hedge the risk since you are lending a smaller amount up front and ensuring the borrower brings funds to closing.

For example, say the total project costs are $200,000 ($150,000 for purchase and $50,000 for rehab). If you were to structure an LTC loan, you would be funding the same percentage of both. At 75 percent LTC, you would lend 75 percent of the purchase and 75 percent of the rehab. This forces the borrower to have funds for both the down payment and the renovation. Some lenders like this approach, as it reduces the risk of funding 100 percent of the purchase and encourages the borrower to start the rehab with their own funds.

These loans require the lender to keep funds available for the remaining portion of the rehab budget. Remember, the borrower is only putting up 25 percent of the rehab, so after they infuse their own capital (with proof), you will need to disburse the remaining funds at a predetermined time during the rehab. This is also known as a rehab draw. We highly recommend setting up a draw process and schedule with the borrower before the loan closes. It's important for both parties to know stipulations of the rehab draw before the loan funds so there is no confusion or delays after the project is in flight.

CONSTRUCTION OR REHAB HOLDBACKS (DRAWS)

Most of our examples reflect what we would consider a basic fix-and-flip deal: a midrange house with cosmetic renovations that likely include new paint, flooring, kitchen, baths, and landscaping. It may involve a little plumbing and electrical that is exposed when walls are opened up, but it will not be a "down to the studs" remodel where the borrower is moving walls, updating all major systems, replacing the roof, windows, structural repairs, or more. For these larger projects where there can be a large six-figure remodel budget, the risk is higher because the value of the property drops the moment the walls are opened up.

One risk-mitigation tool that private lenders can use is holding back some or all of the rehab or construction funds. A holdback refers to the amount of money being borrowed that will be held back at closing, either by the escrow company or the lender directly. This is done to protect the loan by ensuring the project starts off successfully before you release more funds.

Holdbacks are not typically done on smaller-scale projects. In our market, the average cosmetic flip will have a $75,000 to $80,000 rehab budget. If we were to hold back half of that amount and only disburse $40,000 when the property was purchased, we would likely have to give the remaining amount within a few weeks. That's because $40,000 can easily be spent in the first week of a project just on deposits and materials alone. For complex rehabs, however, with larger budgets around $125,000 to $200,000, you may wish to hold some funds back until the borrower has successfully passed certain key milestones. On a basic level, this may be after electrical and plumbing is signed off by a city inspector to verify things were done to code before the drywallers come in and cover everything up.

When investors are required to take draws against the money held back at escrow, it can be done several different ways.

- Draw requests completed using pictures, Facetime video, or on-site visit
- Draw requests completed upon invoices (direct payment to vendors)
- Draw requests completed upon receipt of payment (reimbursement of expenses paid by the borrower)

This is just a quick overview of how holdbacks and draws work at a very high level. For a standard fix-and-flip project, you will likely not need to employ this type of practice. Remember, your goal is to mitigate risk, but you do not want to create an administrative nightmare for your borrower by handcuffing their ability to pay contractors and subs quickly.

PUTTING THE NUMBERS TOGETHER

Let's use some real numbers to better explain each of these metrics and how different lenders might structure their loans.

- **Purchase price:** $150,000
- **Rehab estimate:** $75,000
- **After-repair value:** $300,000
- **Borrower's capital investment:** $75,000 (includes money the borrower put down as earnest money)

If the total project costs are $225,000 and the borrower has $75,000, they will need a loan for approximately $150,000 ($145,000 + approximately $5,000 in closing costs).

The as-is LTV on this loan at $150,000 would be 100 percent LTV and 50 percent LT-ARV.

A beginner private lender may choose not to work with this borrower unless they have additional funds to cover some of the down payment to bring the LTV closer to 75 percent. At 100 percent LTV, this deal has no room for error since the lender does not yet fully understand how to underwrite a fix-and-flip deal and this is their first deal.

A novice lender with a few deals under their belt may choose to proceed with this loan but ask for the borrower to pledge a rental as additional collateral. This rental has some equity in it, and the lender has an attorney familiar with doing loans using more than one property, even if the rental already has a mortgage on it. A borrower will not want to lose one property, let alone two properties, so there is added incentive for them to perform on the loan.

A seasoned lender, who's also flipped a few houses on their own, may choose to take on this deal after vetting the borrower and project in greater detail. However, they may choose a slightly more sophisticated approach of using an LTC loan structure by having the borrower pay 20 percent of the down payment and rehab. If the total project cost is $225,000, the lender may choose to fund 80 percent of the purchase price for $120,000 while the borrower will fund $30,000. The borrower will then utilize the remainder of their funds ($45,000) to start the project while the lender holds back $30,000 to ensure the project gets started quickly.

This is where the flexibility of private lending can be a bit confusing for new lenders. We suggest sticking with very simple loan terms that make sense to you, fit your risk tolerances, and help set up the borrower for success. That is why we had you do the personal assessment at the end of Chapter Three. That assessment will help you build a road map in the face of so many options.

INSURANCE

Hazard Insurance

Traditional lenders tend to have a very specific list of requirements for hazard insurance. If a policy is sent to the lender for underwriting and it does not have adequate coverage, the lender will come back to the borrower or the insurance company with required updates. Having an insurance policy framework in place as a private lender will make your due diligence process go that much faster. In addition, if you work with the same borrower repeatedly, they will be more familiar with your insurance policy and binder requirements and can request quotes that include those limits and coverages you are seeking.

Before we discuss the policy itself, we want to take a moment to touch on the conversation between the potential borrower and you as the lender. First, do not wait until the last minute to get the contact information for the insurance agent or to have the borrower obtain a quote. This will not be a typical homeowner's policy. There are some additional complexities and coverages involved that you need to know about as a lender but may not be familiar with as a typical homeowner. Waiting until the last minute could risk pushing out the closing date, which may halt the entire transaction, as you certainly do not want to fund the loan without proper hazard insurance in place. We once had a property we lent on go up in flames from arson two weeks after we closed the loan—having a policy in place immediately upon loan closing is paramount.

Once you have the borrower's agent/broker identified, it is crucial to send over your contact information and lender requirements, as it may take several days for the insurance professional to find the requested coverage from their providers. The agent/broker will provide you with a document called an "insurance policy quote and binder," which will outline the major details of the property and the coverages being included in that policy. Take time to read the included coverage outlined in the policy quote and request any changes to it as soon as possible. The binder protects you as the lender by allowing you to potentially be paid out first if a claim is made.

You will also inform the agent/broker of the loss-payee clause or mortgagee clause you plan to use for your lending business. This clause informs the insurance company that there is an active lien against the property and provides the contact information for that party. The clause allows the insurance company to inform you as the lender if there are any changes made to the policy, including but not limited to changes in the dwelling limit, the liability limit, claims made against the policy, or cancellation of the policy.

You will also want to provide the agent with the best guess for the date of closing. Hazard policies become effective the day the property changes hands to the borrower, so it is critical for this date to be accurate for coverage. The insurance agent/broker must be notified of any changes to the closing date and be informed as soon as possible that the loan has closed. Most policies are not submitted and bound until the agent/broker has received confirmation of closing from the lender. The last thing you want is to have a house burn down that night, only to find out the policy had not yet been submitted because the insurance agent/broker was not notified that the loan closed a day early and the policy was not set to start until the next day.

As you become more proficient at this, developing a standard process for requesting and evaluating insurance will allow for a smoother transaction. If you leave the conversation to the borrower, they will likely obtain the cheapest policy possible. Chances are those inexpensive policies will not adequately cover the property in the event of certain losses and could in fact be incorrectly written and be found to have no coverage whatsoever in case there is a loss.

Binder Inclusions

Now, what should your binder request include, since we are recommending having one ready to send to the insurance agent? Basic information should be included such as the borrower full legal names(s), the name of the business entity and the state of incorporation if that is the borrower, plus the property address and mailing address for the borrower. Remember, we are lending on non-owner-occupied property. These two addresses should not be the same! Next you should outline your insurance requirements. This can be a bullet point list or a paragraph so long as the information is presented in a clear and concise manner. Let the agent know the loan amount, required policy term (e.g., a twelve-month loan should have a twelve-month coverage), level of acceptable coverage limits for the property, and, if the property is a rental, the amount of loss of rents/income you are requesting to be part of the policy in terms of both time and dollar amounts as well as the minimum liability limit you are requiring for the property. You will also include on this document the loss-payee/mortgagee clause information, including your name, address, and phone number so they can reach out to you as an interested party in the policy.

Keep in mind that the loan amount you are lending to the borrower includes the purchase of the land plus any improvements (any building(s) on the property, also known as dwellings). When you receive insurance quotes, they will only cover the improved structures, not the land. During the global pandemic, the rising cost of materials and services left many properties severely underinsured. You don't want to lend $500,000 and only have the property be insured for $200,000—unless the insurance carrier is able to show that $200,000 is sufficient to rebuild the property.

Establishing Acceptable Coverage Limits

Speaking of rebuilding the property, there are three ways coverage can be assessed to determine how much an insurance company will compensate the insured for a claim.

The first is termed "actual cash value" (ACV). This method of evaluation is based off the cost to repair or replace the damaged property, minus any depreciation of that property. This can be considered the fair market value of that item as it currently stands. For example, if you have ACV coverage for a large flat-screen television in your home, but you file a claim when the television is five years old, the fair market value of a used flat-screen television will be significantly less than what you paid for it (and probably less than the cost of replacing it with a new one). Some properties, due to age or construction, only qualify for ACV coverage, so be aware of what the coverage truly is and how likely you are to be repaid in full in the event of a total loss of the property.

The second is termed "replacement cost coverage" (RCV). The name gives away what they are basing the payout on. The insurance company will pay to replace that item with a similar item according to the cost of that replacement. This method of evaluation does not take into account depreciation of the asset, acquisition, or obsolescence. With the example of a flat-screen television, the insurance company will replace your stolen or destroyed television with a new one of the same kind. In some cases, properties are not insurable for their RCV. An example of this would be a historical home that owes much of its old-world charm to unique materials that do not have an equivalent today. The decision is at the sole discretion of the carrier.

The last and least-discussed term is "functional building value" (FBV). Again, some properties are not eligible for RCV; if this is the case, the next best thing is FBV. FBV states that the property will be replaced or rebuilt with less costly building materials. Insurance professionals consider FBV the next best option to RCV and prefer it over ACV.

Existing structures to the land itself are often covered for ACV only, instead of RCV. This can vary from property to property, depending on the age, construction materials, and history of claims on the property regardless of ownership, but typically insurance carriers will only cover the existing structure for ACV, with any improvements under RCV.

Flood Insurance

You will also need to determine if this property is in a flood zone and what additional coverage might be needed. This can greatly affect the carrying costs, as flood insurance is considerably more expensive than traditional hazard insurance.

Anyone can search what flood zone a property may be in by checking maps located on the FEMA website. The borrower or the insurance agent for the borrower can also check for any sort of elevation certification. This means that the home has been evaluated for its height off the surrounding land. Even if a property was located in a flood zone, it may have an elevation certificate showing the property was raised up or intentionally built up, making damage to the structure from rising water less likely. This would therefore call for a lower flood insurance premium.

An elevation certificate can be obtained in a number of ways and is the responsibility of the borrower to obtain.

1. The seller can share the certificate with the new buyer (your borrower). Some municipalities will require they be recorded with them or made available via public record.
2. A surveyor can provide one if a survey is being done on the property as part of the purchase.
3. Some third-party services online will provide a copy for a nominal fee if they have one.

No matter the method, the insurance broker will need a copy in order to make an accurate quote for home insurance that incorporates both hazard and flood.

You may think this isn't a worry in your area because you aren't near a body of water, but flooding can be an issue anywhere. Low-lying areas can easily flood with too much rain, and normal homeowner's or hazard insurance usually doesn't cover "rising water"—just "falling water." Knowing what flood zone the property is in, how typical flooding is for the area, and if the comparable properties in any of the valuation reports are in the same flood zone is important when evaluating values.

Some lenders won't lend on properties that are in any sort of flood zone, so knowing that very early on helps them avoid wasting time collecting documents or dealing with a borrower they can't work with because of a particular property. Conversely, some borrowers may scoff at the request to order and purchase flood insurance. Just let them know, by law, you are required to have flood insurance on certain properties. If you want to read up on flood insurance regulatory updates, you can visit www.fema.gov/flood-insurance/rules-legislation/laws.

Theft Insurance

Another type of coverage you want to be clear on is theft insurance, specifically under what terms stolen items are covered. Imagine having a borrower purchase all the appliances for a home only to find out that $10,000 worth of appliances were stolen from the home overnight. Make sure you understand under what circumstances theft is covered. For example, does this only include items that have been installed? What about items secured in an area that isn't the property itself (like the contractor's work trailer)? Also, many insurers require the borrower to state if the property will be vacant for an extended amount of time. Say your last tenant moved out mid-month, but the next one does not move in until the beginning of the next month, your borrower would need to inform the insurance company of this gap in occupancy. Most private lenders are only involved in the property for a short term, so they are not likely to see a tenant turnover, but in case this does happen, it is good to know what notifications need to be made. The above is a great example as to why clear, frequent, and routine communication and updates need to occur between borrower and lender.

Liability Insurance

Finally, you will want to establish what sort of liability insurance the policy covers for the landlord. Accidents happen, and something as simple as someone slipping on the stairs while showing the home to a prospective tenant or friend can cause massive financial hardship to your borrower.

If the primary exit strategy of the borrower is to sell the property (fix-and-flip) then there needs to be additional insurance requirements in place to cover incidents that are more likely to happen in a property undergoing renovation. A property in the process of being renovated is most likely vacant as well, so having the proper and adequate insurance coverage for a vacant home undergoing renovations will help ensure adequate financial coverage for your borrower, which means they are more likely to perform on the loan as agreed. If the policy does not reflect that the property is vacant and undergoing renovations, any claims made by the borrower will likely be denied, even if the property were to burn down.

Under this exit strategy, there are two types of policies that a borrower could obtain to have coverage for the property while undergoing renovations. The first is a vacant renovations policy, which covers small renovations to the property such as interior upgrades, cosmetic changes, or replacing the siding or the roof. These changes are nonstructural in nature. When more significant renovations are being done, including structural changes, adding onto the home, moving load-bearing walls, replacing plumbing, electrical, or heating systems, or building an entirely new structure, the borrower will need a builder's risk policy.

ADDITIONAL INSURANCE COVERAGE CONSIDERATIONS

- Determine if the policy will be paid prior to closing by the borrower or if it needs to be paid for at closing. This will affect the borrower's out-of-pocket cash required to close. You will also need to obtain either a proof of payment (if paid prior) or a policy quote (if paid at closing) and make sure the escrow closing agent has a copy to balance their draft settlement statement.
- Find an insurance agent you can work with as a value-add partner who can help you define your specific insurance requirements and insurance binder needs. You can refer them if your borrowers need an agent and, in return, they may be willing to review your insurance binders and policy jackets as needed.
- Consider requiring the borrower to pay for the annual policy in full rather than on a monthly basis. This can help to make sure there is no lapse in coverage.

When it comes to insuring a loan you wish to fund, we recommend you outline your insurance binder and policy coverage requirements in writing as a one-page template you can send to your borrower so they can do the heavy lifting with their agent/broker. Oftentimes, the agent/broker will not work with you without express permission from the borrower/policyholder. As mentioned at the beginning of the book, you should partner with a local insurance agent/broker who is willing to help you come up with proper insurance guidelines for your lending needs and the local market. For example, our agent recommends we have our borrowers obtain $1 million in liability coverage. This is due to the high median home prices in the Greater Seattle market. However, if we were to insure a loan on a property in the Midwest, chances are the liability limit recommendations would be a lot smaller.

OTHER PROPERTY CONSIDERATIONS

As you can see, there are a lot of components to proper due diligence on a property and its correlating project. While you don't need to be an expert in the investment strategy chosen by the borrower, you will still need to familiarize yourself with a variety of metrics used to evaluate deals and effectively protect your loan. When you're unsure how to properly review a property, you will need to lean on your circle of experts to help guide you through the process. In addition to the usual suspects—like real estate agents, insurance agents, and general contractors—we also seek second opinions from friends and acquaintances in our real estate investing network, who can tell us if they'd do the deal themselves or not, and most importantly, why. Talking with another flipper about high-level project metrics can shed a lot of light on a loan we are looking to fund. We also like to ask more than one investor, since we always can stand to learn something new or contemplate a different angle. With every deal analysis, you can become stronger and more informed in your property underwriting.

Chapter 11
UNDERWRITING DEEP DIVE— PAPERWORK

BUSINESS-PURPOSE LENDING CRITERIA

The idea of the loan being for business purposes is woven into a lot of the decisions we make when evaluating a lending opportunity. Depending on the regulations you need to comply with (federal or state), you will find different variations of what is considered "business purpose." If at any point you are unsure about a lending opportunity and whether it can be reasonably considered business purpose, reach out to an attorney familiar with lending. Consumer loans are very regulated and require a significantly higher level of disclosure and possible licensing for a lender. One way many lenders avoid the consumer loan issue is to fund the loan with a business entity as the borrower and not the individual(s) themselves. This method, as mentioned, could require additional legal considerations, but the act of lending to an LLC, partnership, or corporation helps to mitigate some risk associated with the loan being deemed personal in use. The following outlines a few basic criteria to give you some guidance on if a loan can potentially be classified as business purpose.

Non-Owner-Occupied Property (NOO)

This tends to be the first benchmark a lot of lenders look at to establish if this is a loan they can originate under the business-purpose guidelines. There are clear distinctions in lending laws required for owner-occupied (OO) property and non-owner-occupied (NOO) property (investment property). If you are looking to originate a loan on real estate, you need plenty of supporting documentation showing that the borrower currently resides at a separate address and does not plan to occupy the property as their primary residence. We always recommend borrowers complete an NOO letter stating they will not, at any time during the loan, occupy the property or use it for personal use. This will prove helpful in the event a borrower decides to get a bit sneaky and move into the property post-rehab, which would then make it an owner-occupied property. A sample copy of this letter can be found in the supplemental materials at www.biggerpockets.com/lendingbonus.

Written Borrower Statement

Requesting a statement from the borrower that clearly outlines what the money will be used for can also go a long way to proving and supporting a business-purpose loan. This statement needs to be a bit more detailed than "I'm buying this rental house." It should include the address of the property they are acquiring, what their intended purpose is for the property, their current address, what renovations (if any) they are doing to the property, and what their preferred exit strategy might be (rental, fix-and-flip, etc.). The more details they can provide in their own words, the less the business-purpose loan can be challenged.

Some lenders assume they are legally protected by stating the loan is for business or commercial purposes in numerous places within their loan documents. The issue with just having statements embedded within your loan documents is that the borrower could always claim they were not made aware, they did not understand, or they did not see the clauses in question. Having the borrower complete a statement in their own handwriting helps to establish intentions up front and avoids any lack of understanding or potential language or cognitive barriers. We suggest having the borrower complete this as part of the application process in the form of a Business Strategy Letter as well as a form within the loan documents called an Affidavit of Business Use or something similar. Samples of these forms can be found in the supplemental materials at www.biggerpockets .com/lendingbonus.

Business Account Funds Deposit

Lastly, if you require escrow to send funds to a business bank account and not a personal account, it can further support your case that this is a business-purpose loan. Be sure to consult your attorney on the legalities of lending to business entities in your state and how that may affect licensure requirements, disclosure requirements, and usury law. Some states have different provisions if the loan is to an individual as opposed to a business entity. However, there are a few states that have the opposite regulation and ask for a license and/or added disclosures if the borrower is a business entity. When in doubt, contact your local real estate attorney or reach out to a national law firm that specializes in private lending. See the supplemental materials at www.biggerpockets.com/lendingbonus for more information.

TITLE INSURANCE

In Chapter Six: "Compile & Condition," we discussed ordering a preliminary title report, also known as a title commitment. The reason we as lenders want to analyze the title commitment is to review the vesting (ownership) of the subject property, as well as any liens or encumbrances that need to be cleared to proceed with the purchase of the property and the loan to fund the acquisition. We also addressed the need to order a Lender's Title Policy to protect your loan. Here we will discuss title considerations in greater detail so that you have a better understanding of what matters affecting title are necessary for you as a lender to be aware of before funding a loan.

It bears repeating that the topic of title insurance could fill its own book. While we won't dive super deep into all the matters that could affect title and the various ways to transfer deeds of ownership, we will discuss the two basic types of title policies and the components of a title commitment that you need to be concerned with as a lender. Additionally, there are some major issues and title defects that can stop a loan, which you will need to know about in advance. If the title is successfully cleared, you can proceed with funding the loan. Lastly, we'll address a few things you'll want to be aware of while the loan is active in relation to the title of the property.

Title Insurance Policies

There are two types of title insurance you will need to be aware of:

Owner's Policy

This is title insurance a new owner/buyer obtains to protect their claim to the property against fraud, vesting issues, and other unforeseen issues that may affect the validity of the purchase and sale transaction. For example, if you purchase a property with an owner's policy only to find out that the owner on the Purchase and Sale Agreement is, in fact, not the actual legal owner, then the owner's policy helps to protect the buyer against these types of issues.

Unforeseen issues can include deeds completed by persons who are not legally allowed to authorize such transfers of ownership, such as minors, persons of unsound mind, or persons executing an invalid power of attorney. Owner's policies also protect against errors and omissions made by the title company, such as mistakes in the recording of legal documents, fraudulent or forged legal documents like wills or lien releases and deeds, or other forms of fraud not detected prior to the closing.

Lender's Policy

This is title insurance typically required by lenders to safeguard the priority of their mortgage or deed of trust against a property. A Lender's Title Policy also protects against loss or damage associated with title issues or loss of priority of the mortgage or deed of trust. In other words, if you are lending in first position and it appears a lien was placed on the property prior to your loan closing—pushing your loan into a second junior lien position—a lender's policy could help mitigate the risks and losses associated with this loss of priority in lien.

While both policies are technically optional, we require both when lending on purchases. It is critical to have the vested ownership protected by an owner's title policy, and it's imperative to protect your principal loan amount with a lender's policy, in the event of fraud, errors, or omissions that could adversely affect your loan lien position and/or your borrower's legal claim to vested ownership.

There are two different types of lender's policy: standard form (ALTA standard) and ALTA extended. As mentioned in Chapter Six, we always recommend getting the ALTA extended policy. Although it's slightly higher in cost, there are extra provisions and coverages that are beneficial to you as the lender against loss of value in the property—specifically, anything that could affect the ownership or value of the subject property which *is not* found via public records, and which would not be protected under a standard title insurance policy.

For example, if a special assessment for a large dollar amount was placed against the property and not found in public records, this would be covered under an extended policy but not a standard one. In another example, if an unrecorded mechanic's lien was placed against a property and not discovered before the transfer of ownership, this would not be protected by a standard policy but would fall under coverage of an ALTA extended. Mechanic's liens and unrecorded survey and boundary questions are two of the biggest concerns as a lender. For a more detailed explanation of the key coverage exceptions, we suggest you reach out to your local title officer and/or your real estate attorney for clarification.

A final note about title policies: We suggest you always ask ahead of time whether a title company offers ALTA extended. Not all of them do, and it's not fun to find out a few days before close that you will need to switch title companies and obtain a new policy. This could set back closing deadlines and cause some issues with both borrower and seller. While most of the larger title companies will offer extended coverage, many smaller independent title companies will not.

Understanding the Title Commitment

Reviewing your first few title commitments can be a little daunting due to the sheer volume of pages to read and the confusing nature of all the clauses in such a detailed report. While there are many different legal clauses and coverages in a title commitment, here are some of the more important things you'll need to review:

Schedule A

Think of this as the key details of the transaction. The Schedule A part of the title commitment includes the current vested ownership of the property (the seller named on title) and future vested ownership (the borrower as defined by the Purchase and Sale Agreement). It also includes the property address (be sure to review this for accuracy), the purchase price, the loan amount, and the type of coverage being extended to the borrower. Ensure there is both an owner's policy and an ALTA extended policy listed on the commitment.

Schedule B: Part I

This portion of the title commitment traditionally comes in two parts, creatively known as Part I and Part II. Part I lists out any requirements or stipulations for the title commitment. Many of the items here are standard boilerplate requirements and are not specific to the property or borrower itself. You should read through these for your general understanding. After a few loans, you will be able to peruse these quickly, as this section does not vary greatly from deal to deal.

One noteworthy element here is a standard exception associated with states that have legalized marijuana for either medical or recreational use. These states will typically see an exclusion on title related to properties used for legal marijuana activities such as growing, manufacturing, distributing, or selling. Generally speaking, the title company will not insure against properties subject to federal seizure due to the Controlled Substance Act and other federal regulations outlawing marijuana grow and sale operations. While we've never seen this type of issue impact a lender, it's not completely out of the realm of possibility; a lender would need to evaluate this potential risk were the property used in this nature.

Schedule B: Part II

This part of the title policy covers special exceptions to the title insurance commitments—these are any recorded issues that the title company will not insure against. These exceptions can be any liens and encumbrances against the property that need to be either paid off at closing or removed prior to closing. Part II can also include recorded surveys, covenants, easements, and other such property rights and access issues.

We've seen some Schedule Bs with nothing on them and some that are pages long with liens, judgments, deeds, and a litany of other title challenges that would make it difficult to clear before the closing deadline. However, in a purchase transaction, most of the line items on a Schedule B would pertain to the seller and not your borrower; therefore, most of the issues would be paid for out of the sale proceeds at closing and are of little concern to you.

Other Title Commitment Considerations

As mentioned earlier, there are several types of special exceptions under Part II of the title commitment that can prevent a purchase and sale transaction from moving forward to close. Here's a brief summary of the types of issues that are the responsibility of the seller versus those your borrower is required to remedy—and others that are property-specific.

Seller Responsibilities on Schedule B Title Exceptions

Examples of exceptions that would originate with the seller are existing mortgages or deeds of trust and any unpaid property taxes that would need to be paid out of the sale proceeds.

Lis pendens: Another exception you may see is a lis pendens. A lis pendens on the property is a legal action that prevents any sale, transfer of ownership, or further encumbrance of the property until the legal proceedings are settled. In other words, this means the property is not legally available for purchase and the sale could not proceed without the lis pendens being removed.

Code violations: These are another title issue that can affect the sale of a property. Depending on the type of code violation placed against a property, there could be fines, penalties, or work that would need to be completed in order to remove the code violation from title. Often, these issues affect the living condition of the property and present potential health and safety hazards—you want code violations cleared up before the borrower takes possession of the property.

Borrower Responsibilities on Schedule B Title Exceptions

An example of title exceptions that can originate with the borrower is any personal judgments or liens that appear on title because they were recorded publicly and prevent the borrower from acquiring any property without paying off the debts owed.

IRS tax liens: Perhaps one of the biggest issues we've encountered with borrower-liable exceptions is IRS tax liens. Unlike a personal judgment or even a code violation that could be easily removed from title, the IRS is notoriously slow and difficult to make contact with. Therefore, it can be a lengthy and cumbersome task not only to obtain a payoff demand for the final amount owed but also to actually make the payment to the IRS and get the lien removed. This has been a challenge for some of our borrowers and, even with help from the title department, can take weeks or months to settle.

Marital status: Another issue that can potentially affect title would be the borrower's current marital status. We've encountered situations where the borrower is legally separated but the marriage has not been officially dissolved. Since the borrower is still legally married and we reside in a community-property state, we would require the spouse to either quitclaim their rights to the property or become a named borrower or guarantor of the loan. In matters of marital discourse, these issues are not easily solved, and we've often found the spouse uncooperative, halting the purchase of the loan.

Business-entity signors: If the borrower taking title to the subject property is a business entity, proper entity documents will be required by the title department to determine the validity and status of the business as well as to establish how the borrowing entity will sign purchase and sale and loan documents. You should expect to see a supplement to title showing exactly who is required to sign and how they will need to sign. As a general rule, we require all members of a business entity with 20 percent or greater interest to be included as signors of the loan.

Property-Specific Schedule B Title Exceptions

When it comes to the subject property, there may be some special exceptions to be aware of.

Access: Title insurance covers the insured party (you as the lender, in the case of lender's title insurance) for losses related to losing access or right of way to the property itself. This coverage is for the legal right to access the property, not for physically being able to access the property. Being able to access the property directly affects its value and ability to be sold. Therefore, it's important for investors who like to invest in areas with challenging topography or rural areas to pay attention to easement and access to properties. Some properties may share a common driveway before splitting off into individual parcels. Just because a driveway exists does not mean there is legal access to that property, so if you are lending on these types of residences, note if the property has legal access for new tenants or owners. Generally, any easements allowing access to a property are going to be noted in a separate area of the title policy called Schedule B.

Landlocked property is property that cannot be accessed through public thoroughfares, meaning that it is only accessible through a neighbor's lot. A vacant lot that is located behind a strip mall and can only be reached by walking through the mall qualifies as this type of property. Access to a landlocked property or parcel can be challenging for the owner. However, state and federal laws protect the right of property owners to "productive use" of their land, which means the right to gain access to a public road. One way to gain access to a public road is through an easement that grants the right to cross over neighboring land.

Zoning ordinances and government regulations: Zoning ordinances prevent people from using their land in a certain way. Noncompliance with existing ordinances or later discovery of those violations may result in the owner of the property paying a substantial amount of money to cure those defects. A Lender's Title Policy insures against preexisting violations of certain laws, ordinances, and government regulations relating to occupancy, use, or enjoyment of the land; character, dimension, or location of an improvement erected on the land; subdivision of the land; or environmental protection. The policy also covers the policyholder if there is later enforcement of the existing law, ordinance, and government regulation.

Government police power: A Lender's Title Policy also covers the insured if there is an exercise of government police power that is reflected in the public record, but only to the extent that the enforcement is referred to in the recorded notice. These can include things such as zoning laws, building codes, fire codes, and other safety hazards that may be on the property. This process gives a governing body the ability to enforce these rules.

Eminent domain: Eminent domain represents the power by the government, typically exercised by the state, to "take" any personal property for the public good so long as the government provides the private landowner with just compensation. "Taking" occurs through physical appropriation, which is when the government occupies the land in whole or in part (e.g., a law requires apartment building owners to allow private companies to install television lines in buildings), or regulatory taking, which is when a government action affects the value or use of a person's real property. The regulation must deprive the owner of all economic value to be considered "taking" under the doctrine of eminent domain. Regulations that merely decrease the value of the property (i.e., ones that prohibit the property's most beneficial use but still leave an economically viable use of the property), are not considered "taking."

This policy will cover the policyholder if their insured property is "taken" through eminent domain (through physically appropriated or regulatory taking) so long as the exercise of eminent domain is recorded.

Government taking: This is the same taking as described above in eminent domain. However, unlike the government taking through eminent domain, which must be recorded, the taking here does not have to be recorded in order to be covered by the title policy.

Creditor's rights: A Lender's Title Policy will protect the policyholder in the event that the lender's lien of the insured mortgage upon the title is unenforceable or invalid due to a finding of forgery, fraud, undue influence, improper execution of the insured mortgage, or improper filing or recording among other things.

Gap coverage: Title insurance also insures the purchaser's ownership (or a lender's mortgage) as of the date and time of recording of an insured instrument, which is the date on the policy. As we have discussed before, there can be a lag between closing, filing, and recording the lien against the property. This is termed a "gap" in time. If a title defect shows up prior to the new deed of mortgage being filed, gap coverage allows for coverage of that time. A gap period may refer to the span of time in either or both of the following scenarios.

First, there may be a time period between when a document is submitted for recording and when it is actually indexed by the recording office and available for search, usually a matter of days. This means that title commitments and subsequent date-down searches may not include documents that have not yet been indexed. In some states, it is common for transactions to close a day or more before the insured documents can be recorded.

If the title insurance policy is dated as of closing rather than recording, there can also be a gap in coverage because the documents do not take effect until they are actually recorded. Most title insurance policies provide coverage for defects that may arise during the gap period caused by indexing and search availability. However, when a title policy is dated effective at closing rather than recording, a gap-insurance endorsement is added to title insurance to cover any items that may be discovered after the closing date (policy date) and before the recording date.

Invalidity and unenforceability of the mortgage: When a lender sells a mortgage to another entity, the lender usually prepares an assignment of mortgage to the new entity. Ideally that assignment is then recorded in the local municipal public records. An assignment of mortgage gives the loan seller's rights under the mortgage, including the right to foreclose if the borrower doesn't make payments, to the new owner of the loan. An assignment of mortgage serves as proof of the loan's transfer from one party to another. Courts have dismissed some foreclosure cases when the foreclosing party couldn't produce a written assignment. Depending on state law, if the lender doesn't have an assignment or didn't record it at the proper time, the owner of the real property to which the mortgage is attached might be able to challenge the foreclosure on the grounds that the foreclosing party doesn't have the right to foreclose. A Lender's Title Policy protects the policyholder if the assignment of the insured mortgage is found to be invalid or unenforceable or if the assignment in Schedule A fails to vest title free and clear of liens, so long as the assignment is shown in Schedule A.

Lack of priority over other encumbrances, contractual future advances and other assignments: Title coverage ensures that the lien position you have coverage for is accurate and that if other issues with title are discovered, your first lien position is defended or the discovered items can be paid to be removed.

There are other riders and coverages you can have the borrower purchase should you want the additional protection. For example, property types such as condominiums may warrant having some additional insurance for title. The important thing about title is that you understand the risks a particular title policy may have for you as the lender. Remember, private lending is a team sport, so if you have questions, reach out to ask others. Very specific title questions are best answered by a real estate attorney, while general questions about coverage can be handled by the title agent issuing the title insurance.

Post-close title insurance considerations: There are a few things that can affect a lender after the loan is in place and title insurance is ordered. These title issues include mechanic's liens placed against the property after rehab begins, code violations for improperly completed work or health and safety violations, and any of the other special exceptions we covered above that could be levied against the borrower and/or the subject property. The point is that after the loan is in place, there are times where you may need to request a title supplement so that you are aware of any additional exceptions added to the title after your loan funds.

One reason you may want to request a supplement would be when a borrower is requesting a change to the loan, such as an extension or additional funds. There are some things out of the borrower's control during the renovation process, such as supply-chain problems and labor shortages (as seen during the COVID-19 pandemic). They may request an extension to allow for work to be completed. An extension may also be needed if the borrower is keeping the property as a rental but the refinance requirements involve the borrower showing a certain length of time of ownership or income.

If the borrower comes to you and asks for additional funds to complete their project, you might look into why the borrower needs the additional funds and whether it would be worth the risk to extend additional capital. As the lender, you will want to review a current title supplement to ensure nothing new has been added to title that affects your decision-making. If the borrower has a new mechanic's lien on the title because they have not paid the electrical contractor in full, you may choose not to provide more funds until this issue is cleared up.

We're sure this section has brought about more additional questions or concerns than we are able to address here. While we don't want to scare you, it's important we set clear expectations on how title issues can affect your loan both before and after the deal closes. When in doubt, you should always consult your title officer for more clarification. They are the experts in title reports and can help you navigate any title issue that is difficult to discern.

Disclosure Requirements

Private lending operates in this space where we must be compliant on both the federal and state level. While many of the terms that are possible with your loan may be state-specific, some of the disclosures you will have with your loans will come from the federal level, even if you are firmly in the business-purpose lending space. We will run through some of the most common federal disclosures you may want to add to your document arsenal for borrowers, or potential borrowers, to acknowledge as part of your loan process. Be aware that some of these disclosures are not necessary if your loan is well documented to be for business purposes and/or made to a business entity. Again, we want to make sure we stay within those guardrails as much as we can as lenders throughout the loan process. This topic even goes all the way back to our pre-step, Calculate & Evaluate, when we were discussing establishing some loan criteria. Knowing what types of properties, borrowers, and loans require certain disclosures or limits is a large part of establishing your lending parameters.

Equal Credit Opportunity Act (ECOA): The Equal Credit Opportunity Act (Regulation B) applies to any loan that will be in the first lien and that will be used to purchase one- to four-family properties. The good news is that this law is very easy to comply with. It just involves incorporating some consistent practices and possibly some automations into your lending process.

The first part of ECOA requires you to make your borrower aware that they have a right to receive a copy of the appraisal or any other means you used to validate the value of the property, now or in the future. They must receive this disclosure within three days of making the application. To maintain compliance, most lenders will simply have this as part of their application process when the borrower applies for the loan.

The second part of this legislation states that the borrower is entitled to receive a copy of that appraisal at least three days before the loan closes and as soon as it is made available to you as the lender. You can include in your application process the ability for the borrower to opt out of the timing of this legislation. That would allow you to close the loan before the three-day period between when the appraisal is received and the time of closing. On the flip side, if the loan is denied, you can just give them the valuation documents at the time the loan is denied.

Despite its requirements, the ECOA isn't necessarily concerned with the appraisal component of the loan. It is mostly in place to oversee discrimination in lending and to ensure lenders aren't discriminating against any of the protected classes: race, skin color, religion, national origin, sex, marital status, age, and sources of income. Further complicating things in the private lending space is that borrowers are technically business entities. Often in private lending you are evaluating so many things about the borrower that are quantitative in nature, such as asset levels or income, that you aren't in the business of evaluating much about the person who would be a partner in that business entity.

The last part of ECOA requires an adverse-action letter. This is a letter you will supply, if the borrower requests it, that outlines if the loan has been denied or revoked. It is not required if a borrower wants additional money to finish the project or is in default. This applies to any application that is received, no matter what the purpose of the loan was originally. The adverse-action letter outlines why the loan was denied, and if it was based upon information contained in their credit report, they have the right to request the reason for denial.

Home Mortgage Disclosure Act (HMDA): This disclosure just started applying to business-purpose loans recently, but it is limited to certain types of business-purpose loans. The Home Mortgage Disclosure Act requires certain financial institutions to collect, report, and disclose information about their mortgage lending activity. The information collected by the lender centers around the demographics of the borrower and the loan type; it applies to any loan used to secure any residential property that is one to four units, regardless of owner occupancy. There is a threshold limit that a lender must surpass for the legislation to apply, so it is best to reach out to your attorney to find out what that threshold may be for your business, and then establish procedures to comply with that law. If you are using the 1003 application as your standard loan application (or some version of it), it asks all the relevant information required by HMDA. Most lenders who only fund a handful of deals a year will not be subject to these regulatory reporting requirements. If you plan to scale your lending, then you will need to consider the minimum loan threshold required for HDMA reporting. It would also be a good idea to look at a loan origination software specific to private lenders that allows for data collection and reporting.

Fair Credit Reporting Act: This act covers a borrower's credit report if you decide to pull one on them. It does apply to business-purpose loans, but it is ultimately focused on having the authorizations in place to pull credit on an individual. Even if your borrower is a business entity, if you are going to ask the principal of the business entity for a personal guaranty, then you will need authorization from those principals as individuals.

Service Members Civil Relief Act: The last federal disclosure is the Service Members Civil Relief Act, which offers financial protections for someone if they are called to active duty. They must change from off duty or reserve duty to active duty in order for this to apply. For example, if you have a borrower whom you funded a loan for while they were active duty, this set of protections would not apply to them. The borrower must request this relief instead the lender, as the lender is not responsible for trying to figure out if the borrower has changed military status during the course of the loan. An easy way to make this simpler is asking every applicant if they have any affiliation with the military. If they say yes, you can get some clarification on if they are a veteran, active duty, reserves, etc. The implications of this act center around forbearance and foreclosure mitigation, rather than you as a lender having to actively do something different for a borrower who *may* be covered by this loan and is paying as agreed.

Privacy Policies

Anyone who has ever purchased a home probably remembers the seemingly endless stream of documents and disclosures to sign. The good news is that private lending in the non-owner-occupied, business-purpose loan space generally comes with significantly fewer disclosure requirements, and many are considered best practice versus legally required. However, it is worth noting that offering the appropriate disclosures, even as best practice, can give you additional options for the loan and support any challenge about the loan made in court later on.

The first thing both parties may not even think about is a privacy disclosure. As a lender, you are collecting some very sensitive information about the borrower. This one is therefore especially important to have early on—as early as the application process. The privacy policy outlines what you as a lender can do with the information provided, who you may disclose certain information to about the loan or the borrower, and what parties the information can be shared with and for what purpose. This is crucial for a few reasons. First, you may want to disclose some sensitive information to additional people in your professional network, such as your CPA to review complicated tax returns, or your personal lawyer to validate some items on the application. Second, if you ever want to sell your loan, the buyer of the loan will want to know a lot of key details about the borrower paying on the loan. Having the ability to disclose that information to a potential buyer of the loan makes that possible; without it, you are likely violating privacy laws. Make this a part of every loan application, even if the loan doesn't close. You may need to share information during the Compile & Condition step, but then may ultimately uncover a reason why you are not comfortable with moving forward with the loan.

Foreclosure Considerations

The first question most new and aspiring private lenders ask is "What happens when the borrower doesn't pay you back?" It's natural to be consumed by the negative consequences associated with large investments like private lending. As you've learned by now, in the event the borrower goes into default, there is a chance you will go into a foreclosure proceeding. The following provides an overview of the foreclosure process, should it occur.

Judicial vs. nonjudicial foreclosure: If you must go into a foreclosure proceeding, it's important to understand the difference between judicial and non-judicial foreclosures—and how that difference affects your overall investment in terms of time and money.

Mortgage states typically allow for non-judicial foreclosure, which is an expedited process for foreclosure proceedings. This means the foreclosure happens outside of the court system. This contrasts with a judicial foreclosure process, which relies heavily on the court to foreclose on the property. In a judicial foreclosure, there will be scheduled motions and hearings. You will have to work with the court schedule in that municipality, and as we saw during the pandemic, some courts can shut down entirely for weeks or months at a time. In states that use deeds of trust, the foreclosure process may involve notification that the foreclosure process is commencing.

Some states allow you to opt for judicial versus non-judicial foreclosure, despite the title of the lien instrument. In California, for example, the non-judicial foreclosure process can take four to five months if the foreclosure is not contested. If the foreclosure is contested, it could take considerably longer to get the capital back out of a property. Meanwhile, in Texas, a non-judicial foreclosure can happen in just twenty-five days!

Non-judicial foreclosure is an easier process to go through in the sense that you record certain documents against the property, set a sale date, and then move forward with the sale. There are notice and publication requirements that go with this option, so having an attorney knowledgeable about the foreclosure process can really help should a foreclosure be necessary.

Timeline considerations: It may be worth investigating what the foreclosure process and timeline is before you close on the loan. Knowing the timeline you may face if the worst-case scenario happens may force you to be more cautious and judicious in your due diligence. As scary as foreclosure may sound, it is a surprisingly straightforward process with clear steps and requirements. Being aware of what timelines you may be facing in the event of foreclosure can also give you an idea of how long to deploy your capital. If the borrower is asking for a twelve-month loan, but the foreclosure process usually takes twelve months in your state, you need to evaluate whether you need this chunk of money for anything else in the next twenty-four months. Therefore, when pricing your loans, think about the length of time the loan may be out, as well as the legal costs associated with foreclosure so you can prepare for the worst and hope for the best with every loan.

Communication is key: Foreclosure is usually the result of two parties not communicating well enough to find an alternative. There are often hurt feelings, exchanges of unpleasant words, and, eventually, a total loss of trust. The borrower may even intentionally damage the property or stop working on it at a crucial point. Imagine a property that sits vacant for four months while foreclosure proceedings are happening, but the borrower removed a large section of the roof to repair something and hasn't put it back—four months of the elements leaking into a home, along with the wildlife that are likely to move in, can significantly impact the value of the property.

This whole foreclosure discussion really aims to answer one question: If this does go downhill and you have to foreclose, how fast can you as a lender get out of this, and can you sustain the loss or the time that it's going to take to go through that process?

Paperwork Considerations

We cannot express how important paperwork is to the entire private lending process. It's obvious that loan documents represent a critical piece of legal paperwork, but there are many other important documents to collect, create, record, and, ultimately, understand in their entirety. This is not an exercise a lender can breeze through.

Think of a detective evaluating a crime scene. The most incriminating evidence is not always super apparent. It can be a tiny bloodstain on the back of a door, undetectable without a magnifying glass. Or it can be the faint printed words on a piece of paper that can only be seen when held up to the sunlight.

Your detailed review and analysis of the documents you receive and prepare should never be overlooked. Small details such as the lack of an interest rate on your promissory note could make it difficult to foreclose, should you need to. Or the title closing process could be hugely complicated by not noticing the borrower is married on the title report, and is therefore subject to community property laws unless the spouse agrees to remove their interest from the title. All the little details in your paperwork matter and need to be examined closely.

This will be a work in progress as you grow in experience. In the meantime, build enough time into your loan funding process to allow you to become acquainted with the many forms of documentation needed in private lending. This will ensure you never feel rushed into funding a loan without fully identifying and understanding the potential risks that could threaten your capital investment.

Chapter 12
BRINGING IT FULL CIRCLE— LEND TO LIVE

If you made it to the final pages of this book with only a few puzzled looks and you haven't gone cross-eyed yet from all the new terminology, the risk factors, and the numerous considerations—well done! You likely have a laundry list of new questions you want to ask from new people you will need to meet. We know it's a lot to take in, because we've been in your shoes before. Trust us when we say these feelings of apprehension, hopefully blended with some excitement about getting started, will be short-lived as you start the process and begin your journey to discovering more.

While it may seem like the entire C.P.R. lending method is extremely involved and time-consuming (and in the beginning, it might be), it will be a relatively low volume of work compared to the time frame in which your loan is passively earning interest after the funded deal. Some lenders we speak to have their processes and systems down so tight that they are able to fund deals within a couple days (assuming title is already opened and clear of exceptions). Others, including us, typically take a few hours a week on a loan over the course of about ten to fourteen days, give or take. The most exciting aspect to this schedule is that you get to set the timelines. You can also do all of these tasks from anywhere you want! Has your attorney prepared your loan docs and they are ready for review, but you're at the beach? No sweat—review them on your iPad! The borrower just sent you over a bunch of documents you requested, but you're tired? You've got this—read them from your phone in bed (just make sure you're not too tired to review them with a fine-tooth comb). The point here is that with a little hard work up front and a "lifelong learner" mindset, you can build the private lending practice of your own choosing.

We have a friend, Mike, who sold his medical-alert business that he built from the ground up. After years of the long, arduous work required of a start-up, he decided he would take the proceeds from the sale of his business and begin private lending as a form of passive investing, while traveling to all fifty states with his wife and their two dogs in an RV. It sounds like a dream to us, and it most certainly was to him.

Zach, another novice lender friend of ours, wanted to start private lending after he'd house-hacked his first investment property, a duplex he occupied on one side and rented out on the other. He quickly realized the strong demand for private lending, and after falling in love with the real estate investing space, he decided to jump in and lend out money to other active real estate investors while he continued working his day job in the tech industry. Loving the freedom that private lending gave him, Zach set a goal to scale his small, independent private lending practice into an active business so he could quit his day job within a year. He's only 27 and has a vision (and business plan) to replace his W-2 income with private lending within the next eighteen months and is hopeful he can make a family business out of it by encouraging his fiancée to join him shortly thereafter.

Alex started in private lending as a way to quit her day job as a chemistry professor so she could have the freedom to travel and see her spouse for weeks at a time while he was stationed abroad. After being an active-duty military spouse for twenty years, Alex vowed she'd never be away from him for extended periods of time anymore.

To us, freedom is everything. We assume it's important to you as well, which is why you picked up this book in the first place. For some, freedom is time. For others, freedom is family. However you choose to define freedom, private lending can most certainly support this vision. Beth's mom used to say all the time, "You never get to heaven and wish you had worked more. You always wish you'd had more time with loved ones, checked things off your bucket list, and enjoyed the wonders of life." You don't have to believe in heaven; you just have to believe that your time is valuable and know exactly what priorities come first in your world.

Speaking of time, we are providing extra resources, forms, and supplemental materials (www.biggerpockets.com/lendingbonus) that will help speed up the learning curve and onboarding into private lending. We encourage you to leverage these resource and tools as much as possible. As we have alluded quite a few times in these pages, the virtual team you create will be immensely helpful in your journey. Establish your network quickly and with the strongest players you can find and always remember that you do not have to go it alone in private lending. In fact, the team you assemble will be paramount in giving you the freedom you so desire. Aside from real estate and private lending legal support, you can create a really powerful support team with your local title officer, insurance agent, and other real estate professionals.

It will also be important to surround yourself with a strong private lending network. Learning from other private lenders can be a powerful source of knowledge and a great way to gain different perspectives. We encourage you to join some of the national associations, social groups, and other forums to connect with other private lenders. We're partial to the Lend2Live: Private Lending Lessons Facebook group we manage because it has thousands of members representing aspiring, new, and scaling private lenders like yourself. No question is too dumb and the depth of knowledge from the group is profound.

Private lending is a team sport. Regardless of whether you want to invest passively or create an active private lending business, your network really is your net worth. This book, or any book on private lending for that matter, will never be the Holy Grail. We outline the system needed to create repeatable steps for successful completion of the private loan life cycle, but it's the people and roles you insert into each of those steps that will make you the most successful.

We would like to be part of your success story in private lending too! Once you get started, we would love to hear about your journey. Let us know your challenges, what goals you've set for yourself, and most of all, the successful first loan you complete. We're just an email away. You can reach us at alexandbeth@lend2live.com. We look forward to celebrating your many successes to come!

ACKNOWLEDGMENTS

We would like to acknowledge the people who have helped us in our journey in their own ways. This work is the product of many individuals doing many different things; every story and experience leaves a mark, even if its origin cannot be traced to the proper author. For the nameless, know every interaction you have with another leaves an impression. Those impressions are not without merit or worth!

First, we want to thank BiggerPockets for allowing this book to be made. We felt so strongly that the story of private lending needed to be told to allow more people to invest passively and live actively. The publishing team heard what we had built and made it better. This has become more than we dreamed, and we're honored to be part of BiggerPockets' mission to help people reach their financial goals.

As we mentioned, this book was not done alone. We received guidance and insight from many people—mostly other women in real estate! Melissa Martorella from Geraci LLP provided a lot of insight into the regulatory and title process. Her way of breaking down complex topics into layperson's terms has been invaluable. We often reached out to Geraci LLP with questions as laws and regulations changed, and we continue to do so. Elaine Eugenio, the hardest-working woman in insurance, jumped in time and time again to add clarification to insurance processes, policies, and coverages that speak to lenders and investors alike.

Alex specifically would like to acknowledge and thank her father, who never lived to see this book come to fruition but who fully inspired its creation. An author and educator in his own right, he was an example for not only how to get concepts across but also how to provide real-life examples for application. His desire to invest in real estate to support his family led to weekends mowing lawns at rentals, tours of prospective properties, and lessons in ways to think creatively and critically. He never met a stranger, would talk to anyone about anything, and could be heard before he was seen. Those characteristics were passed down to Alex and shaped who she became. In addition, Alex would like to thank her chosen family for picking up the slack on days when lending matters took over. Your support allowed her the freedom to work on a project that came from a place of passion and a desire to help. The very action of family coming together to help one another is the true measure of success. They embody the phrase "people before profit" every day with their generous spirits.

Beth would like to again thank her husband, Matt, for giving her this amazing life and for always being a source of inspiration, laughter, and positivity. She'd also like to thank Gary Schuetz for his infinite wisdom, friendship, and guidance throughout the years. Together, Gary and Matt taught Beth everything there is to know about private lending, and then some. She is grateful to her children, Caleb and Rachel, for making her strive for something greater than herself. And to Mia, who taught Beth how to be a better mom; she is awed by your strength, insightfulness, and caring for others. You are her personal confidant and the center of this blended family.

Lastly, Beth is grateful to Alex—"for carrying me across the finish line more than once when I couldn't do it myself." And Alex is grateful to Beth—"we are orcas and together we can lead the entire pod."

More from
BiggerPockets Publishing

The Book on Tax Strategies for the Savvy Real Estate Investor

Taxes! Boring and irritating, right? Perhaps. But if you want to succeed in real estate, your tax strategy will play a huge role in how fast you grow. A great tax strategy can save you thousands of dollars a year. A bad strategy could land you in legal trouble. With *The Book on Tax Strategies for the Savvy Real Estate Investor*, you'll find ways to deduct more, invest smarter, and pay far less to the IRS!

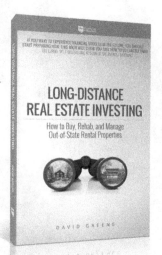

Long–Distance Real Estate Investing

Don't let your location dictate your financial freedom: Live where you want, and invest anywhere it makes sense! The rules, technology, and markets have changed: No longer are you forced to invest only in your backyard. In *Long–Distance Real Estate Investing*, learn an in-depth strategy to build profitable rental portfolios through buying, managing, and flipping out-of-state properties, from real estate investor and agent David Greene.

If you enjoyed this book, we hope you'll take a moment to check out some of the other great material BiggerPockets offers. Whether you crave freedom or stability, a backup plan, or passive income, BiggerPockets empowers you to live life on your own terms through real estate investing. Find the information, inspiration, and tools you need to dive right into the world of real estate investing with confidence.

Sign up today—it's free! Visit www.BiggerPockets.com
Find our books at www.BiggerPockets.com/store

Recession-Proof Real Estate Investing

Take any recession in stride, and never be intimidated by a market shift again. In this book, accomplished investor J Scott dives into the theory of economic cycles and the real-world strategies for harnessing them to your advantage. With clear instructions for every type of investor, this easy-to-follow guide will show you how to make money during all of the market's twists and turns—whether during an economic recession or at any other point in the economic cycle. You'll never look at your real estate business the same way again!

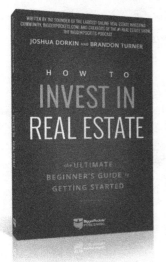

How to Invest in Real Estate: The Ultimate Beginner's Guide to Getting Started

Two of the biggest names in the real estate world teamed up to write the most comprehensive manual ever written on getting started in the lucrative business of real estate investing. Joshua Dorkin and Brandon Turner give you an insider's look at the many different real estate niches and strategies so that you can find which one works best for you, your resources, and your goals.

More from
BiggerPockets Publishing

The Book on Flipping Houses
Written by active real estate investor and fix-and-flipper J Scott, this book contains more than 300 pages of step-by-step training, perfect for both the complete newbie and the seasoned pro looking to build a house-flipping business. Whatever your skill level, this book will teach you everything you need to know to build a profitable business and start living the life of your dreams.

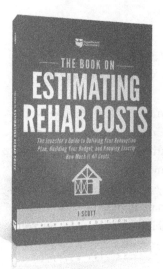

The Book on Estimating Rehab Costs
Learn detailed tips, tricks, and tactics to accurately budget nearly any house flipping project from expert fix-and-flipper J Scott. Whether you are preparing to walk through your very first rehab project or you're an experienced home flipper, this handbook will be your guide to identifying renovation projects, creating a scope of work, and staying on budget to ensure a timely profit!

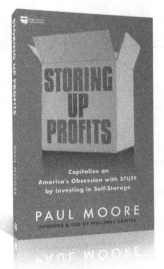

CONNECT WITH BIGGERPOCKETS

and Become Successful in Your Real Estate Business Today!

Facebook
/BiggerPockets

Instagram
@BiggerPockets

Twitter
@BiggerPockets

LinkedIn
/company/Bigger
Pockets

Website
BiggerPockets.com

CPSIA information can be obtained
at www.ICGtesting.com
Printed in the USA
JSHW062122080722
27721JS00005B/5